CONVERSATIONS REGARDING THE FATALISTIC OUTLOOK OF THE COMMON MAN

by Kuzhali Manickavel

Blaft Publications Pvt. Ltd.
4/192 Ellaiamman Koil St., Neelankarai, Chennai 600115 India
http://blaft.com

Some of the pieces in this book originally appeared in different versions in other publications.

Earlier versions of the following pieces appeared in a column in *The New Indian Express* from January–July 2010: 'Fucking Hipsters!! I Hate How You Make Me Feel!' (original title 'Are These Hipsters Not Slow Joggers?'), 'Life Is Very Confusing Dears' (original title 'The Un-Understanding List'), 'I Am A Boss Babe and These are My Boss Babe Pants!!! (original title 'Those Costly Inner You-Yous'), 'Great White Hope', 'Fuck Yeah I'm a Complan Boy!!! ' (original title 'Health Drink Junkie Mutants'), 'I Love You But I Hate You!!!' (original title 'Are the Spider Monkeys on Drugs'), 'Let's All Take Drugs!!!' (original title 'Should Mickey Tell Donald to Put Some Pants On'), 'Tragedy of Poverty in Our Society!!!' (original title 'The Thin Line between Bargaining and Lunacy'), 'The Gee Oh Gee! Wow' (original title 'Who's the Gee Oh Gee'), 'Don't Even Talk to Me Right Now Oh My God' (original title 'Hello Don't Just Hang Up on Me'), 'Let's Make Fun of Other People's English!' (original title 'Open the Windows, Let the Air Force Come In'), 'Bad Words are Bad!' (original title 'Run for Cover You Onion Eggplant Lentil'), 'I Bet You Don't Remember Who Snooki Is Cos I Sure Don't!' (original title 'The Importance of Seeing Snooki'), 'Remember When We Were All Friends on Facebook!' (original title 'What if She's Stalking Me?'), and 'I Watch Indian Cinema!!!' (original title 'One Tight Slap and the Woman Fell in Love').

An earlier version of 'A Cyclone and a Flood' (original title 'Conversations During a Cyclone and a Flood') was published by Dog Oil Press, 2008.

An earlier version of 'It's Raining Babies in Bollywood Oh Wow!!!' (original title 'Why I Can't Think of Anything to Write About Bollywood') appeared in *The Big Indian Picture*, 2012.

Earlier versions of the following pieces appeared in a column in *The Swaddle* from May–October 2019: 'Rat Crocodile Princess', 'Best Friends', 'Good and Bad', 'The F Word', 'Big Kids', 'Marriage', 'Writing Stories', 'Aadhi', 'Paruppu Keerai', 'Be Better', 'The Girl', and 'The Dress'.

Niira Radia's dialogue in 'Lobbying with Niira Radia!! Wow!!' is taken from the transcript of the 'Radia Tapes' published in *Outlook* magazine and elsewhere.

ISBN 978-93-80636-51-1

Cover design by Radha Sunder

Printed at Sudarsan Graphics

For S

Table of Contents

Good morning
Happy Rose Day

No Cholera Here

No Cholera Here

Let's Make Fun of Other People's English!!!

K: So I ran into an old lecturer from college—

S: Oh I love it when people meet their old lecturers! Did she hug you and cry? Did you both have slow-motion college flashback? Was it like the Raymond's ads?

K: Now that you mention it, I think she did want to cry a little.

S: Because she remembered you and was overcome by golden memories from the evergreen pastures of her golden memories?

K: No, because I actually ran into her. As in I accidentally knocked her down some stairs and she may have concussion and stuff.

S: Oh nice!

K: But I totally remembered her! I was like 'Ma'am, you remember me?' and she was like 'Why should I remember you? Who said I should remember your face?'

S: It's a valid question bro.

K: I remember her because every time she came into class, she would say 'Come on girls, open the windows! Let the air force come in.'

S: That is amazing.

K: And I would always think, wouldn't that be the best thing? If you opened the windows and these fabulous Air Force men just started leaping gracefully into the room? Sometimes I would picture the Air Force men wearing little sailor outfits and jumping through the windows while that song Chandralekha from *Thiruda Thiruda* played in the background.

S: I can totally see that happening.

K: It was the best class ever. I can't remember what class it was exactly but it was the best.

S: I had a teacher who would tell us to stop oscillating in the hallways. We never saw her, we just heard her voice. We'd be standing there and suddenly this voice would say 'Girls! Why you are oscillating in the hallways?' I mean how do you even answer a question like that? 'No ma'am, we're not oscillating ma'am'? 'Sorry ma'am, we'll not oscillate again ma'am'?

K: Did I ever tell you about my teacher who would say 'I say you get out!' even when we were outside?

S: So confusing.

K: It really was. Because we wouldn't know where to go, you know? How do you 'get out' when you're already outside?

S: It's a loaded philosophical metaphor.

K: I remember this one girl had a theory that maybe we were supposed to go back inside and then go outside again but we could never test this.

S: Why not?

K: Because this teacher didn't actually want us to go anywhere, she just liked saying 'I say you get out!' So if we tried to move, she'd get even angrier and say 'Where are you going? You are going for a walk? You think this is fish market?' And I'd be like, why would anyone go for a walk in a fish market?

S: OK I have to go. I just remembered I had something on the stove and then I came to talk to you and now my kitchen is probably on fire.

K: Open those windows I say! Let the Air Force come in!

It's Raining Babies in Bollywood Oh Wow!!!

1.

D: Why don't you write about a Bollywood movie and make a lot of references to obscure Japanese cinema and use words like 'post-colonialism' and 'gender tropes'?

K: I don't know what a 'trope' is.

D: I don't think you need to know what it means, you just have to throw it around liberally while writing about something you've seen recently.

K: That would be *Bal Brahmachari*, *Maa*, *Kangan* and *Krodh*. I watched them all at the same time.

D: OK. So maybe don't write about that.

K: I had no idea what was happening. In any of the movies.

D: It's weird that you're watching these movies when you can't actually understand Hindi.

K: It's not weird though.

D: You know when they say something in Hindi? And you can't understand what they're saying because it's in Hindi? And you watch the whole movie anyway?

K: Yeah?

D: Yeah, that's weird.

K: How about I write something like 'Why I Love Bollywood Even Though I Can't Understand Hindi and Don't Really Know What Anyone Is Saying'.

D: I think you should write something called 'Bollywood Post-Colonial Perspectives Kurosawa Gender Tropes'.

K: But I don't know what a trope is!! Or a Kurosawa.

D: Then write something mean about white people but with Bollywood and colloquial Tamil.

K: You're not helping.

D: Write a story then. Your usual what-the-fuck stuff but in Bollywood.

K: I'm going to talk to someone else who isn't you.

D: Write about a dead girl watching a Bollywood movie. And there are insects. Eating her left eye. AND IT'S RAINING BABIES!!! Hello?

2.

R: Write about how you deleted all the Bon Iver I gave you to make room for your Munni Badnaam remixes. Write about how you told me that you thought Bon Iver was Bon Jovi.

K: They are both Bon-Bon, it's an honest mistake!

R: Your taste in music is gross.

K: Why are you so racist against Bollywood?

R: Why are you the only person on the planet looking for a lofi trap remix of 'Don't Touch My Ghaghariya'?

K: Did I mention that I found this Trini-chutney remix of 'Show Me Your Jalwa'? I can send—

R: Good-bye.

3.

A: You should write about that time on Masterchef when Dalvinder won something and then everyone began to move in an alarming manner and they said it was a Bollywood dance and it made us so embarrassed for them.

K: And they made that noise.

A: Right, that weird falsetto police siren thing.

K: I actually thought they were doing an ethnic Australian dance. Then they said it was a Bollywood dance and now I want to know what Bollywood movie had people going round and round like pigeons while making siren noises.

A: I think it's from *Alice in Wonderland.* The 1999 version. The cook does something similar when the Duchess sings that song about beating her boy when he sneezes. By the by, have you seen the *So You Think You Can Dance* Bollywood segments?

K: No.

A: You should.

K: I'm scared to.

A: Dude, you should totally watch them. Open a clip now on YouTube.

K: OK, hang on, let me just—aw what the actual fuck you guys.

A: Whatwhatwhat?

K: There is a dude with a big blue dot on his forehead and he's dressed like Aladdin.

A: OK don't watch that. Close it and don't watch it.

K: Maybe I should just find out what a trope is and write that Gender Bollywood Post-Colonial Kurosawa thing.

A: A trope is a kind of fish, no? I think it is. I think I ate some once.

4.

S: You HAVE to write about how some people in this one number country watch Bollywood ironically. Write about how that's a thing.

K: That's when you act like you like Bollywood but you actually don't but you act like you do to prove how much you don't. Right?

S: Kinda.

K: Why isn't that called lying?

S: Actually you should write about how some people really do like Bollywood and act like they don't and then act like they do to prove that they don't. When they actually do.

K: What does irony mean anyway? Is it like a trope?

S: Or you could write about how when you're watching *Hum* and enjoying like anything some asshole will ask if you're *really* watching it.

K: As opposed to artificially watching it?

S: As opposed to watching 'something good'. Like *Slumdog Millionaire.*

K: You wouldn't know what a trope is, would you?

S: It's a riddle, isn't it? Or a cave made of tarpaulin.

5.

N: I read with great interest your recent post on the actress Jayanthi.

K: I wrote a post on the actress Jayanthi?

N: I don't know if I've mentioned this but when I was in India—

K: You've mentioned it. Repeatedly.

N: And I was such a great fan of the cinema there. Great food, great people. So colourful and REAL, you know? Such authentic energy.

K: Who is actress Jayanthi?

N: You just wrote about her.

K: I wrote about Gandhi Jayanthi.

N: OK. And is that someone different?

K: Little bit, yah.

N: Member of the Gandhi family perhaps?

K: Sure, why not.

N: I am quite familiar with them of course.

K: You are fucking amazing, you know that?

6.

K: So a trope is, and I quote from the indisputable Wikipedia, 'the use of figurative language in literature, or a figure of speech in which words are used in a sense different from their literal meaning.'

S: So what's a gender trope then?

K: It's all what I just said except with genders in it.

S: What does that mean?

K: I don't know. I felt a lot better when I thought a trope was a fish.

S: So how are you going to link this to Bollywood?

K: Well I thought about it a lot and I've decided to call the piece 'Post-Colonial Perspectives and Gender Tropes in Bollywood and Also Kurosawa and Also White People Are So White.'

S: And?

K: And the actual piece will be about this dead girl watching a Bollywood movie and there are insects eating her left eye and it's raining babies.

S: Why is it raining babies?

K: Because of racism.

S: And why are the insects only eating the left eye?

K: Also because of racism.

S: This entire thing is a terrible idea.

K: Ya.

S: DO IT!

K: YAAAAS!

Music Makes My Lyf Rule!!!

K: I'm not doing phone terrorism what the fuck.

S: Calling me eight million times a day and putting on the MunniBadnaamSong is phone terrorism.

K: Who would do something creepy and weird like that?

S: YOU would.

K: I don't understand why you keep saying this.

S: Because the calls come from your phone and I can hear you singing in the background.

K: I'd really love to ask a white person what they think of that song. Do you know any white people?

S: Why don't you look for some on the internet?

K: That's such a great idea actually.

S: You should hang up and go find white people on the internet and not talk on the phone.

K: OK, imma go find some.

S: By the by,

K: Yes, what man? Come on, tell fastly.

S: By the by, if you call me again with that song I will come over there and shove your phone up your nose.

K: Ew.

S: Seriously.

K: OK.

* * *

K: I can't find any white people on the internet! I googled 'where can I find white people' and they said there are single Russian ladies near me but they didn't say where! I think they were lying.

S: NO!

K: YES! I also googled the English translation for MunniBadnaamSong. Did you know that Munni Badnaam Hui means 'Munni goes infamous'?

S: Is that the right translation?

K: It was on the internet so it must be right. Munni goes infamous.

S: Is that like going hungry? Is the song about famine?

K: I actually thought the song was about almonds. Doesn't 'badnaam' mean almond?

S: I think that's 'badaam'.

K: That's not the same thing?

S: Meh maybe it is.

K: Sounds same only, no? Munni Badaam hui. Munni Badnaam Hui. See? Same only.

S: OK, I'm going now bai.

K: Maybe 'badnaam' is a bad almond. Maybe the song is about food adulteration. Hello? Hello? Bro.

* * *

S: Did someone die? Because I can't think of any other justifiable reason for you to be calling me at this time unless someone is dead or the Americans have invaded.

K: I want to know something. In the MunniBadnaamSong,

S: No.

K: There's this line that apparently means 'Became cinema hall for you darling'.

S: I SAID NO!

K: I'm curious to know if that is a sexual metaphor or is it symbolic of the fascination that our country has for the cinema combined with the objectification of Woman or is it a reflection of the fatalistic outlook of the common man?

S: Why don't you go fuck yourself?

K: There's also this line that goes 'Hai jama ishq da ishq da parcha re', only he doesn't say 'ishq', he says 'isk'. Like you know how some people say deospray is iskisk? 'Why you smell so bad?' 'Oh I forgot to do iskisk today' Like that he says. I don't think he means deospray though.

S: I'm hanging up now.

K: Why?

S: Because I am going to come over there and set you on fire.

K: What fire? Hey you better not come over here I'm not wearing any pants. Ah fuck.

GhettoDawg BlingBling

K: So I guess you've been wondering where I've been.

S: Not really.

K: I've been writing the screenplay for my movie!

S: Your movie?

K: *GhettoDawg BlingBling: The Rise of Kevin.*

S: Who the fuck is Kevin?

K: He's the one that rises.

S: You're not serious.

K: I'm totally serious! I have identified the secret ingredient that makes Indian movies win Oscars.

S: Samurais!

K: No.

K: Conflict diamonds!

S: No.

K: Samurais who eat conflict diamonds!

K: Poverty. Poverty wins us Oscars.

S: A movie about Indian poverty. What a totally new and unique idea. I don't think anyone has ever done that before.

K: My movie will be about American poverty. With singing and dancing.

S: What do you know about American poverty?

K: It's the reverse of certain kinds of Indian wealthiness. Like some rich Indians wear black Metallica t-shirts and jeans. So do poor Americans. Some rich Indians believe they are poor Americans. So do poor Americans.

S: This is probably a very silly question but does this movie have a story?

K: Well it has a guy and this guy has a dream. And then Kevin rises.

S: That's it?

K: Ya. I mean, that's like having a story, right?

S: What is his dream?

K: Whose dream?

S: The guy who isn't Kevin.

K: Oh! Um… something to do with baseball maybe?

S: I think you need to work on the story a little. I feel a story is somehow integral to a movie.

K: Who said.

S: I mean, just try it. What happens if my movie has a story.

K: Sounds shady as fuck.

S: Take it as a challenge dear.

* * *

S: Well?

K: I didn't think of a story yet but I wrote the theme song for the movie. It's called *GhettoDawg BlingBling: The Rise of Kevin—Take It to the Streets and Drop the Beat 'Murica The Shep Pettibone Remix.*

S: I think you can only say that if Shep Pettibone actually remixed it though.

K: That's a person??

S: What did you think it was?

K: I thought it was just something you can call your remix if you want. OK so it's *GhettoDawg BlingBling: The Rise of Kevin—Take It to the Streets and Drop the Beat 'Murica.*

S: I mean it's catchier now at least.

K: I'm going to sing it for you now.

S: No.

K: Wickiewickiewickiewickie. That's the record scratching. Wickiewickiewickie. Wickiewickie. Wickie.

S: Please don't do this to me.

K: GhettoDawg BlingBling Blingie Blingie BlingBling GhettoDawg BlingBling Blingie Blingie BlingBling. What do you think?

S: Blingie Blingie BlingBling?

K: Yes.

S: Oh fuck you it's running through my head now.

K: YOU LOVE IT

* * *

K: Don't even think of it as help.

S: Vendaam.

K: Think of it as telling me what you think my movie story should be.

S: Valikithu.

K: And then telling me what to do.

S: Azhuthituven!

K: So we have the guy who isn't Kevin. He has a dream to play baseball and win… whatever it is they win in baseball. I want to say an Emmy.

S: Superbowl pa.

K: No no I don't like all this bowl and all. He wants to win an Emmy in baseball.

S: Appram?

K: So he starts practicing dance in the garage that he works at. Throwing head back and all.

S: Why isn't he practicing baseball?

K: Then he begins going to clubs at night and dancing, throwing his head back and all. And people are like, Oh my God you are amazing, who are you?

S: I am Kevin.

K: And he goes… actually fuck that, nobody asks him that.

S: You do realize that you need to have a Kevin Rising at some point.

K: So then he goes to New York for the audition.

S: And he walks into the BalletModernJazz Dance School of Dancie Dance. And they all look at his greasy face and overalls and laugh at him in the New York languages.

K: YES!

S: And then he starts dancing and they go oh my God, you are now our top banana dancer.

K: THIS IS AMAZING! Then he goes to Europe for the competition.

S: I don't think they have Kevins in Europe, do they?

K: Why do you keep talking about Kevin?

S: He's supposed to rise, remember? And what about the baseball?

K: Kevin is really starting to constrict my creative expression bro.

S: WHAT ABOUT THE BASEBALL YOU FUCK

* * *

K: What if Kevin is like a giant… something.

S: That rises?

K: Yes.

S: I feel a lot would depend on what Kevin is.

K: He is the product of a cruel world. He is vulnerable and sensitive and damaged and broken.

S: And fragile. And scarred.

K: YES SCARRED

S: Maybe Kevin is a Rebel.

K: Like a white dude in a leather jacket who doesn't care about anything and smokes!

S: And he wears jean shorts.

K: No dude.

S: With a plastic belt. And the most delicate white socks you ever saw.

K: With downy blonde hair covering his whitewhite legs.

S: HIS DOWNY BLONDE HAIR SHIMMERS IN THE WIND LIKE BAD QUALITY PLASTIC

K: How does a Kevin like this rise though? What's at stake?

S: Bro I'm tired.

K: Think of Kevin and tell me what you see.

S: I WANT TO GO HOME

K: TELL ME WHAT YOU SEE

* * *

K: Hmm. Yeah I don't like any of that.

S: But that's what baseball is.

K: I feel like baseball should be about horses. And cowboy hats. And everything is in slow motion.

S: Dude you can't say that's baseball when baseball is actually a thing that exists which isn't that.

K: You're not the boss of me.

S: Dude.

K: Are you saying that I, as a middle-aged brown lady who has no idea what baseball is, am not allowed to write about baseball??

S: You can't just call something baseball because you like it better that way!

K: YOU ARE STEPPING ON THE NOSE OF MY CREATIVE EXPRESSION

S: Bro—

K: NO ONE LETS ME WRITE ABOUT ANYTHING

S: Bro—

K: I AM BEING OPPRESSED

S: OK.

K: Gosh this making a movie thing is tiring.

S: OK, so what do we have so far. We have a theme song. We have a movie title. We have a dude who dances in a garage and is not Kevin. And we have Kevin with the downy blonde leg hair and delicate white socks.

K: That feels like a good story to me bro.

S: To be honest, I'm not sure what else we can do here.

K: I'M EXHAUSTED

S: And who knows, maybe people will appreciate our use of baseball in the story even if it isn't 100% accurate.

K: You can't restrict art like that. WE ARE NOT COMMUNISTS.

S: But I have a Mao Zedong t-shirt.

K: SOMETIMES WE ARE COMMUNISTS

The Real India Is Really Really Real

S: And he said, people like you don't realize this, but the best food in this country is on the streets.

K: Ew.

S: He says it's on the streets, in the heart of this nation, in the Real In—

K: Don't.

S: in The Real—

K: DON'T FUCKING SAY IT!

S: The Real India.

K: Oh you fuck.

S: Then he's like, I know this because I've sat with manual labourers and asked them to share their food with me.

K: What kind of asshole asks manual labourers to share their food?? I hope they said no.

S: I KNOW! I was like, why the fuck would you do that? And he goes, because I'm a guy that knows how to treat everyone the same.

K: I HATE THIS SO MUCH!

S: He's was like, I am one of them!! And I said you're really, really not though.

K: Uh oh.

S: So obviously some kind of Poverty Olympics started. He was like, I went to school in a toilet, my family lived in a bucket and ate plastic bags, how can you say I'm not like manual labourers?

K: HOW CAN YOU DO IT.

S: He also said his family never went abroad for holidays as a child, and that he only got his own bike when he was in college. So… that happened.

K: Is an auto driver his best friend? I bet an auto driver is his best friend.

S: You have to be willing to go into the really uncomfortable areas, he says. You have to really live there, with the people.

K: Bro, I'd be super offended if someone came into my area just so they could tell the internet how uncomfortable it was.

S: So then I was like, OK dear, you win all the Poverty Olympics and all the poor people. And I probably should have left it at that.

K: You didn't.

S: But then I said, you obviously haven't eaten the best beef fry in Chennai though.

K: Oh you fucker.

S: Naturally he goes of course I have, I know the owner, he's my friend. So I go, not the touristy one, the real beef fry place.

K: The touristy one! Ouchie.

S: So then he's like haha pretty sure I go to the real one haha. So I say, well then you know it's beyond that tea stall built from old tires. And he goes, yeah I know that place, the owner is my friend.

K: What a nice public fellow this dude is.

S: Then I say, and you go past the brain fry stall and past the railway track where they brew country liquor out of used bars of Hamam soap and Tiger biscuits? Until you find the marijuana guy who hides the weed inside bunches of sirukeerai and has no face? He's like, yeah I know him. He's my friend.

K: I wish I had as many friends as he does.

S: Then I was like, you're talking about the one that's in deeeeep interior Parrys, in an area infested with large quantities of poor people, under a haunted bridge that is constantly guarded by vicious minorities. Right? And he says yeah.

K: WHY ISN'T THE MEDIA TALKING ABOUT THE VICIOUS MINORITIES!

S: So I say, great! That's the place! Let's go then.

K: And?

S: And he said he would but he was wearing his good shoes and he didn't want them to get stolen.

K: Was he planning on taking them off?

S: No, but he felt like they would get stolen anyway. Also, he had already had a bath and the katcha mutcha would make him dirty.

K: FUCK YOU KATCHA MUTCHA! FUCK YOU SO HARD.

S: And then he made some kind of joke about usually covering himself in penicillin before going to places 'like that'.

K: That must have been super funny.

S: I was like aw come on, we can catch straight bus there. And he said he didn't like traveling by bus with women because he was always expected to 'do something' when she got felt up or something.

K: That is annoying, you have to admit.

S: And that was it basically. When I left he was talking about road safety for cyclists, but I think it was more for the reflective-sunglasses-no-Indian-culture-spandex-shorts cyclists. Not for the barefoot-family-on-a-Hercules cyclists.

K: Well I mean those dudes haven't had road safety all this time, why would they suddenly need it now?

S: And that's why I got the text asking me to 'cool it with the communism' because it was making people uncomfortable. Which is true, I was being pretty gross.

K: I mean, I was uncomfortable just listening to that.

S: Anyway I will now go to an obscure and dangerous tea kadai because I know the owner and he is my friend. I will take biscuit from bottle without asking. I will eat a greasy, unlabelled packet of deep-fried things like I know what these deep-friend things are. Then, I will drink the tea and look deep into the distance like I am part of this attractive but darkly mysterious world.

K: Can I come?

S: They said you're not allowed.

K: Why?

S: Because.

K: Eh, that's fair.

Bad Words Are So Bad

S: Did that abusive child harass you in the road again?

K: What is his problem? I have never done anything to him ever!

S: Didn't you tell him his parents were fattening him up because they wanted to eat him one day?

K: I may have mentioned that in passing.

S: And isn't he scared to eat with his parents now? And doesn't he have panic attacks whenever he sees a spoon?

K: Yeah whatever. Anyway, now I can't walk past his house without him verbally abusing me.

S: Dude he's six.

K: You have no idea what comes out of that kid's mouth. Today he kept calling me an eggplant and an onion. Like he was going Hey Eggplant, Hey Onion, Hey Eggplant, Hey Onion.

S: Maybe he's hungry?

K: So I said what do you think you are, a big lentil?

S: A big lentil?

K: It sounds better in Tamil.

S: Such intense food-based abuse bro.

K: Ask me what the kid says.

S: What did he say?

K: He called me a bloody Indian!

S: That is fucking hilarious.

K: I know! I'm like, you can't call me a bloody Indian, you stupid abusive Indian kid!

S: It's so weird when Indians call other Indians bloody Indians.

K: India is the one place where an Indian should be able to walk down the road without having someone call them a bloody Indian.

S: Does he even know what he's saying?

K: I don't think so. And he was doing a little hip shake so it was like this terrible song and dance number. And then he started getting creative and going Bloody Bloody Indian, Bloody Bloody Eggplant, Bloody Bloody Onion.

S: It's not a great song bro.

K: Then I was thinking. What is a bloody Indian anyway? An Indian covered with blood? An Indian who spontaneously bleeds? An Indian who induces spontaneous bleeding in other people?

S: I saw a movie like that once.

K: Really?

S: Yeah, it was like all these people started bleeding all over everything for some reason, I can't remember why.

K: Anyway, then I thought maybe Bloody Indian was code for something. So I went online—

S: What do you do when you can't go online? Just curious.

K: I get really sad and I want to kill myself. Anyway, so I go online and start generating anagrams. And one of the anagrams for Bloody Indian is Bad Idli Onion. OK, maybe it was 'Idly', like Idle-Idly. But I'm going with Idli, like Sambar-Idli. I'm going to call him that next time.

S: You're going to call the abusive kid sambar-idli?

K: No, Bad Idli Onion. It's not a very good idea.

S: Have you tried making friends with this child?

K: Ew no. I dump puffed rice on his head though.

S: Bro.

K: He likes it! We actually hang out most afternoons and I just dump stuff on his head.

S: And sometimes he verbally abuses you.

K: It's a complicated relationship.

S: You go man lamp oil.

K: You go man! Why me?

S: I was translating 'poda velakenne' you ass.

K: Oh my god.

S: Yeah.

K: I LOVE IT

S: Yes you do.

Baby You Can Drive My Green Volvo Lol Jk No You Can't Fuck Off

S: Oh my God!

K: I know!

S: She kept telling everyone in college you had AIDS. And everyone believed her!

K: I know!

S: Why she is calling you? What does it mean when people who hate you that much call you? Should you be scared? Because I'm really scared right now actually.

K: As far as I can tell, she found out that I have no job and no husband and that made her so exceedingly happy she just HAD to get my number and call me up and tell me about how she heard I have no job and no husband.

S: Many people call me for the same reasons. It seems to make them very happy.

K: Anyway, I figured this was a good time to ask her why she hated me so much. Considering she didn't even know me.

S: What did she say?

K: She said, and I quote, 'Well basically it was because you were so arrogant.' So I asked her what I had done that was so arrogant. And she said well basically you walked with a very arrogant manner.

S: I mean, she's not wrong.

K: Then we had a very strange conversation because she started talking about her Volvo.

S: So?

K: Well she pronounced Volvo in a very interesting way.

S: Did it sound like she was saying 'chiropractor'?

K: It sounded like she was saying 'vulva'.

S: Oh my god.

K: You can imagine my confusion when she informed me that it was a nice dark green and she was really excited about the upholstery and sound system.

S: That would definitely be confusing.

K: So I tried to clarify this, because I am stupid. And then we had this very tedious back and forth that went 'I thought you said vulva!' 'Volvo only I said.' 'Vulva. Not Volvo.' 'Volvo only.' 'Vulva! Vulva!' 'Yeah, Volvo. That's what I said.' So I decided to make things worse by spelling it out for her.

S: And?

K: And she said there was no need to say such obscene and arrogant words to her because I was obviously jealous of her Volvo.

S: Did she mean her car or—

K: I thought it better not to ask.

S: Is 'elbow' an obscene and arrogant word too?

K: Not sure. It might be if it's a woman's elbow.

S: Uterus?

K: Oh definitely. That's definitely obscene and arrogant.

S: Worse than fallopian tube?

K: Way worse.

S: This is very confusing. How are we supposed to know what words are obscene and arrogant? Is there a guidebook or something?

K: There should be, no? Anyway, so she got really pissed off at me for being obscene and arrogant to her, although she was very pleased at my Volvo-envy. And before she hung up on me she said I was a gay also.

S: What's a gay also?

K: I think it's those hammocks that wealthy Indians use in the summertime.

S: Oh how nice! I've seen gay alsos in ads for insurance and whitening creams!

K: Yeah. Not sure why she called me that though.

S: I'm never saying the word Volvo ever again. There's just too much drama attached to it now.

K: Ya I think I will just say foreign carcar like everyone else.

Rat Crocodile Princess

Niece: Should I tell you something so scary?

K: You absolutely should.

N: One day there was a rat.

K: Is that it?

N: And he had fourteen teeths. In his ear.

K: That must have been painful.

N: Ya. And he had a gun. And he was a crocodile also.

K: I thought you said he was a rat.

N: He was a rat crocodile.

K: That's really confusing.

N: And he had a penis. Because he was a boy.

K: OK.

N: I don't have a penis.

K: That's true, you don't.

N: Because I'm a girl.

K: Well, not exactly.

N: Hm?

K: I mean some girls have penises. And some boys have vaginas. Is that confusing? If it's confusing then I didn't tell you this okay?

N: Can I be a boy?

K: Sure. Would you like to be?

N: Not right now.

K: Well that's fine. You can be whatever you want.

N: Can I be a house?

K: You can't be a house though.

N: A shoe rack?

K: You can't be a shoe rack. Actually there a lot of things you can't be, sorry bro.

N: Hm?

K: Let's get back to the rat crocodile, shall we?

N: He was a princess. Can a boy be a princess?

K: I guess so. What do you think?

N: I think if he has his own crown then it's fine.

K: That seems fair.

N: Then you know what happened? The rat crocodile died.

K: Aw.

N: And his teeths grew into… elbows.

K: So he had fourteen elbows. Coming out of his ear.

N: Yes.

K: Wouldn't that be really uncomfortable? Or does it not matter because he was dead?

N: He became alive again.

K: Oh yay! How did he become alive again?

N: He… he just got up.

K: OK. So it wasn't like he was actually sleeping and not dead at all?

N: No he was dead.

K: OK.

N: Because there was so much blood. And bones.

K: Right.

N: Then the rat crocodile he ate up the girl.

K: Why is this sounding like some '80s horror movie? Wait. What girl?

N: The girl.

K: Why couldn't he eat a banana?

N: He ate all the girls. And then he went swimming. And he had a coffee.

K: Was this rat crocodile an investment banker?

N: Ya. Hm?

K: And when you say he ate all the girls, you mean like every single girl in the world.

N: Ya.

K: Did they give him indigestion?

N: No but he felt sad because then he didn't have any friends.

K: Because all his friends were girls.

N: Ya.

K: And, for reasons best known to himself, he ate all the girls.

N: You know why he was a princess?

K: Please tell me.

N: Because he liked to eat sparkles. And that's how he got all sparkly.

K: Does a princess have to be sparkly?

N: Yes. And they also have to have a pet.

K: Aw, what kind of pet?

N: A bus.

K: Do you think you could draw this rat crocodile princess?

N: Ya.

K: Excellent. Sally forth with paper and coloured pencils.

N: It's going to be so scary.

K: I shall gird my loins.

* * *

K: So I was wondering if you could walk me through this picture. Because it seems very complicated, there's definitely a lot going on here.

N: Ya.

K: So right here, we seem to have… a mountain range? Or a chainsaw possibly?

N: It's elbows.

K: So then this box-like structure is… an ear?

N: Nose.

K: And this is his… face?

N: Ya.

K: So why is the nose outside his face?

N: Because I put it there.

K: That seems fair.

N: Say what this is.

K: It's a…. deflated egg? With feet?

N: It's a shoe rack.

K: Why is there a shoe rack— actually you know what? Never mind. Tell me what this fountain of rainbows is coming from his…

N: Mouth.

K: Is he throwing up? Are those his teeth? Are you going to tell me it's actually a piano or an artistic expression of regret?

N: He's eating sparkles.

K: Oh right.

N: And he's throwing up.

K: OK. And so this entire being is half rat and half crocodile… how exactly?

N: His back is a rat. And his feet are crocodiles, see?

K: Ah. And when you say they are crocodiles, I see that each foot is an actual crocodile. Unless those are slabs of cheese.

N: It's crocodiles.

K: This is, by far, the best rat crocodile princess I have seen today.

N: I know.

K: So is it a boy or a girl? I don't think we resolved that.

N: He's both.

K: As are we all.

N: Except when he's a house.

K: Right. Remind me to talk to you about that one day.

N: You want my rat crocodile princess picture?

K: Oh awesome, can I have it?

N: No.

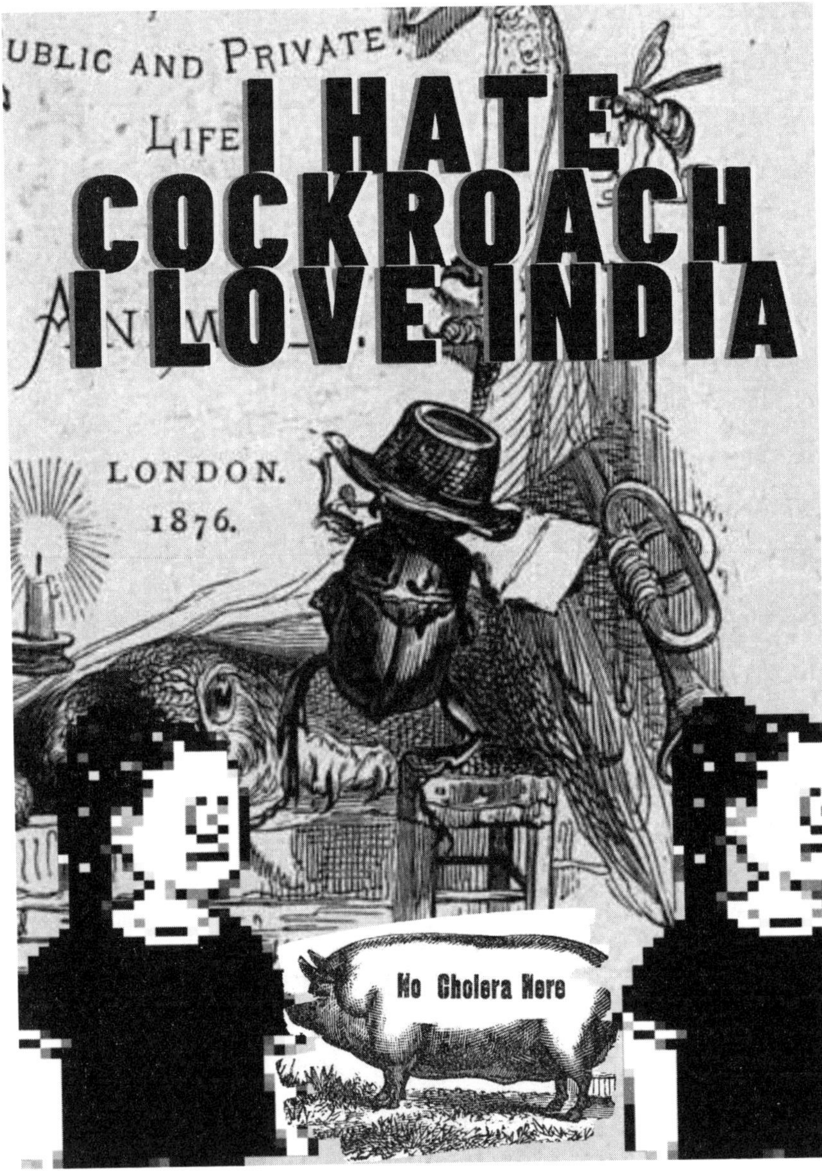
UBLIC AND PRIVATE
LIFE
I HATE
COCKROACH
I LOVE INDIA
LONDON.
1876.
No Cholera Here

Government Offices Make Us Sad :(

K: Guess who just got back from Government Office excursion?

S: So that's where you've been all day! The Gee Oh!

K: I am the original gangster of the Gee Oh.

S: You're the Gee Oh Gee.

K: Yeah you know me!

S: Who's the Gee Oh Gee?

K: Yeah you know me!

S: OK enough. What games did you play today? Did you play Run Up And Down And Up And Down The Building Signature Hunt?

K: No, that was last time. And a very invigorating game it was too because one person absolutely refused to sign anything unless I bought them samosa and tea, sang their personal top ten hits of MGR while standing on one leg, and promised to bring them four bottles of authentic Andhra mango pickle.

S: So what was today's game?

K: First we played Repeat After Me Because You Are Stupid.

S: I've never played that!

K: It's definitely one of the Old Skool games. The esteemed Gee Oh Official yawns at your kazillion papers. Then he says 'You need to get attestation from two freshwater ducks that are on their way to Latvia.'

S: Then?

K: Then he looks at you and says very slowly, 'You need to get? Come on, tell me?'

S: Oh! It's like filling in the blanks!

K: It really does wonders for your self-esteem to be an adult and sit there while another adult talks to you like you are a three-year old that eats glue.

S: It is a very long game?

K: It really is. We were playing for about an hour before we finally got to 'Two freshwater ducks that are on their way to? Come on come on say me? Lat-vi-a. Very good.'

S: You played that the whole day?

K: No, after that we had a very dramatic session of You Don't Have A Pen?!

S: That game scares me. So intense. So many emotions.

K: I think some of our most powerful dramatic actors work in the Gee Oh and they only display their full artistic prowess when they find out you don't have a pen. This one was just like Sivaji, very powerful emoting.

S: These are the people who can win us Oscars!

K: He kept saying, 'You are an educated person? You don't have a pen?' Then the burden of this became too much for him so he started telling this to everyone who passed by. Then it turned into an interactive theater piece.

S: Wow, what was that like?

K: Half the people said I didn't have a pen because I was arrogant and the other half said it was because my family was arrogant. I didn't realize there was such a strong connection between arrogance and not having a pen.

S: Do you have a pen now.

K: Yes.

S: LIAR

K: Why would I lie about having a pen?

S: DO YOU HAVE A PEN NOW DEMON

K: No! What the fuck, leave me alone!

S: I've always thought I would make a good exorcist. Or like a... what's the word? Like a—

K: Priest?

S: No.

K: Manthravaathi?

S: Beekeeper! That's the one. Always thought I would be a good beekeeper.

K: I thought you didn't like bees?

S: WHO DOESN'T LIKE BEES! Oh wait, you're right. I don't like bees.

K: We started this conversation with government office shenanigans and now we have come to bees. So that's interesting.

S: It's not actually.

K: Yeah.

The Telephone Makes It Easy for Us To Communicate With Our Friends!!!

The Conversation Terrorist: You don't want to talk to me. I can tell.

S: I've literally been talking to you for the past 6 hours when there was nothing to talk about in the first place.

The Conversation Terrorist: You never want to talk to me. You talk to everyone else but you never talk to me.

S: It's humanly impossible for this conversation to go on. If we keep going, someone will go crazy and start eating their own face. And by someone I mean me.

The Conversation Terrorist: See? You don't want to talk to me.

14 hours later

The Conversation Terrorist: So. Tell me something.

S: I feel like killing myself. Repeatedly.

The Conversation Terrorist: You're acting like you don't want to talk to me.

3 days later

S: I need to go to the bathroom.

The Conversation Terrorist: You can take your phone into the bathroom, no? Unless you don't want to talk to me.

S: No no. You're right. I've always wanted you to hear me pee.

The Conversation Terrorist: Don't drop the phone down the toilet. If you do, I'll think you don't want to talk to me.

S: One day, possibly very soon, I will die. Who will you talk to then?

The Conversation Terrorist: No idea. You have any suggestions?

S: Hang on, let me hook you up with someone. You can call them whenever.

The next day

K: OHAI!!!

The Conversation Terrorist: It's 3 in the morning.

K: Why didn't you call me? You were supposed to call me bro.

The Conversation Terrorist: It's 3 in the morning.

K: Is it? I don't have any clocks in my house.

The Conversation Terrorist: Why not?

K: I don't believe in time. I think it's a CIA plot. Anyway why I called you means...

8 seconds later

The Conversation Terrorist: Hello?

K: Yes?

The Conversation Terrorist: Why aren't you saying anything? Why you called means?

K: Oh right! Why I called means I wanted to warn you about what happens sometimes when people call me.

The Conversation Terrorist: You put your phone in the mixie.

K: I only did that once. What happens is sometimes people call me and all their major internal organs just spontaneously fall out of their body. Has that ever happened to you?

The Conversation Terrorist: Why do you say such things? I think maybe a lot of people find it very irritating when you say things like this. Especially when you call at 3 in the morning and tell them.

K: I think maybe a lot of people can go fuck themselves.

The Conversation Terrorist: I think you only use such language because you really don't want to talk to me.

K: Fuck Fuck Fuck Fuck Fuck.

The Conversation Terrorist: See?

K: Fuckity fuckity fuckfuckfuck.

16 seconds later

The Conversation Terrorist: Hello?

K: I hung up on you.

The Conversation Terrorist: I thought it got cut.

K: I heard you do a lot of drugs, is this true?

The Conversation Terrorist: Chee, I never do such things.

K: Do you eat fetuses?

The Conversation Terrorist: What?

K: You must never eat a fetus. You must also never shake your uterus. If you don't have a uterus, you must never go and shake someone else's uterus.

The Conversation Terrorist: Did you say 'eat a fetus'?

K: Do you take Crocin?

The Conversation Terrorist: Sometimes if I have headache I—

K: That means you do drugs. I'm talking on the phone with a crack whore.

The Conversation Terrorist: I'm not a— Hello? Hello?

20 seconds later

K: I hung up again. I think maybe you don't want to talk to me because you're a crack whore. Is this true?

The Conversation Terrorist: I think maybe—

K: I heard that all your ancestors had non-consensual sex with dead trees. Is this true? I won't judge you but I do want to say that consensual sex is always the best kind of sex. You may want to share that with your people.

The Conversation Terrorist: Are you saying bad things about my family?

K: I feel like you don't really want to talk to me but you are because you want to have non-consensual sex with the dead trees on my ancestral properties.

The Conversation Terrorist: I—

K: My ancestral property trees are not dead yet! I don't have any ancestral property trees!

The Conversation Terrorist: OK, this is—

K: WHY DON'T YOU WANT TO TALK TO ME?

The Conversation Terrorist: I really don't—

K: WHY?

The Conversation Terrorist: I—

K: WHY WHY WHY WHY WHY? Hello? Lisa? Have you ever considered changing your name to Lisa? Hello?

* * *

S: I regret to inform you that The Conversation Terrorist's number seems to have changed.

K: You think they're hiding because they don't want to talk to me?

S: Yes.

K: Do you want to talk to me?

S: No.

K: Why though? Hello? Ah fuck you anyway though.

Writing Stories

N: You want help?

K: No.

N: I can help. I'm good at writing stories.

K: I don't think you can help with this one.

N: Why? I know lots of words. And also animals.

K: This doesn't have any animals in it. And the words are weird enough as it is.

N: Put 'piano' in it. Put 'cabbage'.

K: You want me to just randomly mention pianos and cabbage in my story.

N: Ya.

K: That's not a bad idea actually.

N: Then say there was a mosquito. And his name is Suresh.

K: I'm not adding a mosquito named Suresh in my story.

N: Why?

K: Because I feel I have to draw the line somewhere and that seems like a good place to draw it.

N: What about a elephant?

K: No.

N: Two elephant.

K: Dude if you don't leave me alone I'm going to shave your head.

N: Write, once there was a elephant. And a shoe rack. Write.

K: I'm not putting a shoe rack in my story.

N: Why?

K: Because… well I guess I could.

N: What kind of story is it?

K: I have no idea.

N: Is it so scary story?

K: I guess not so much a scary story as a… not-making-any-sense story?

N: What happens when it's so much not making sense?

K: That usually means it's done.

N: Does it have cockroach in it?

K: Not yet.

N: You should put one.

K: Will you leave me alone if I do?

N: Ya. And a crocodile.

K: OK. 'The fading light on the old ancestral home looked like a cockroach and also like a crocodile.'

N: It's nice. Now put elephant.

K: Actually maybe we should… oh.

N: What happened to all the words?

K: I… don't know. Did I just delete everything?

N: What means delete.

K: I made them disappear. I can bring them back though, no big deal. Like this. Like… this. This… oh my god what the f— Come back!

N: What happened?

K: I just deleted everything!

N: Why?

K: Because I'm stupid!

N: You said stupid.

K: Oh my God what did I just do!

N: You said stupid.

K: Oh. My. God.

N: Yesterday I said bum.

K: Dude that was almost 3000 words!

N: No.

K: Yes!

N: You can't write so many words.

K: Um, I just did. Before I deleted them all. Like an idio… syncracy.

N: Where you got so many words but.

K: This is not the time for your weird questions.

N: Why?

K: I was supposed to submit that tomorrow Oh My God.

N: Why you always say oh my god.

K: Oh my hecking god!

N: What's a hecking god?

K: I have to try and get this back, away with you little dude, go do something.

N: I write another story. I be very quiet.

K: Please gods give me back my story please please please.

N: Write 'oh my god'.

* * *

N: Why you lying down?

K: Because I just lost a 3000 word story somewhere in the wilds of my computer and I can't find it.

N: Hm?

K: All the words are gone little dude.

N: Because you made them disappear.

K: Yes.

N: Because you are stupid.

K: I totally am.

N: I wrote a story.

K: Aw, for me? To help me out?

N: No, it's for me. I read it to you?

K: Why not.

N: Once upon a time there was a shoe rack and a elephant.

K: An elephant.

N: Ya, an a elephant. They were best friends. They ate curd rice and chips. One day the shoe rack died.

K: How does a shoe rack die?

N: He got sick.

K: How does that happen?

N: Then the elephant was so angry. And he stepped on the cockroach.

K: What cockroach?

N: That one that was there. And the elephant died.

K: There is so much death in your stories.

N: You like it?

K: I liked the curd rice and chips part.

N: What was your story?

K: It was probably about unhappy people who have weird things happen to them. I can't really remember actually.

N: You should write about shoe rack.

K: Maybe you're right.

N: I can draw one for you.

K: OK, let's assess my current situation, shall we? I have a submission deadline tomorrow and I no longer have a story to submit.

N: Amma bought chips yesterday.

K: Really?

N: Ya. There's curd also.

K: Your Amma doesn't like you eating curd rice and chips.

N: Ya but you lost all the words. And there's chips.

K: I can't argue with any of that. OK, come on little dude, let's have curd rice and chips and then take a nap.

N: You can have my story if you want.

K: Really?

N: Ya.

K: That's really sweet, thanks little dude.

N: It's OK, it's not so good.

NO ONE LIKES MY COLOUR DRESS
MOOD OFF
#feelingsad

I Watch Indian Cinema!!!

K: I'm having a Man With The Pipe Movie Marathon.

S: Is that porn? You're doing a porn marathon?

K: No, it's all these old movies that have The Man With The Pipe in them. You know, that guy with the gray hair, suspenders, moustache, pipe. He sort of just stands on large winding staircases and says 'Jolly good!' or 'I say you get out!'

S: Oh right! I saw a movie where this dude also stole radioactive things that looked like tubelights and hid them in his briefcase.

K: I saw a movie where he kept whipping his wife with his belt.

S: His pants didn't fall down?

K: No, he's got suspenders, remember?

S: So he's smart AND sexy!

K: There was this scene where he's whipping his wife and she's hugging his legs and he's trying to shake her off, like 'Get off me so I can whip you better.'

S: I've never understood that, why would you grab the legs of someone who wants to whip you to death?

K: I know, right? And you know what the Leg-Hugging Woman says? She says 'You can beat me, kick me, even kill me. But please just tell me what I did to deserve this.'

S: That is fucking amazing.

K: Then things get very complicated. First the Hero slaps the Heroine because she's arrogant and speaks English and wears pants. Then she falls in love with him and starts wearing saris.

S: That ALWAYS happens when you slap someone. One Tight Slap—Oh I Love You—Oh I Am Wearing Sari.

K: Then The Man With The Pipe slaps the Heroine because he's like, how can you let the Hero slap you, you're supposed to be arrogant and speaking English.

S: And hello, where are your pants?

K: Exactly. And then the Hero slaps the Heroine again because he's like how can you let The Man With The Pipe slap you, only I'm allowed to slap you because I love you.

S: And in between all this the Leg-Hugging Woman got whipped with a belt.

K: Yes. Then after being attacked by something that looked like a plastic pink flamingo, The Man With The Pipe and the Hero decided to be friends. So they were shaking hands and The Man With The Pipe was saying 'Jolly good!' and the Heroine and the Leg-Hugging Woman were smiling at each other like 'Thank God nobody's beating us right now!'

S: That sounds a lot like the radioactive-tubelights-in-the-briefcase movie.

K: Maybe it's the same movie! Was there a party scene with all these malnourished people holding glasses of juice and looking really sad?

S: No, but the Heroine could play the piano without actually touching the keys. It was amazing.

K: I'm so conflicted bro. On the one hand, I love these movies because I love them. On the other hand, these movies also make me talk like a feminist.

S: EEEWWW

K: I KNOW

S: Why don't you read an improving book instead?

K: Why don't you go fuck yourself.

Let's All Take Drugs!!!

K: Happy Bird Day!

S: It's not my birthday.

K: Not birthday, Bird Day. It's your Happy Bird Day. It's your day of happy birds. Birds are just like you and me except they all have wings. Or do they?

S: Imagine if you actually took drugs.

K: I did take drugs bro! I am a drug taker! I take all the drugs!

S: You didn't though.

K: I sat next to someone who did drugs.

S: I'm not sure weed counts.

K: Being high is extremely exhausting for me. And disorientating. Disorienticorating.

S: You're not high though.

K: Why is 'orient' in the word 'disorient'? Does it mean that all oriental people are lost? Isn't that racist?

S: How long are you going to do this?

K: I NEED THE DRUGS GIMME SOMETHING FOR THE PAIN MAN!!

* * *

K: Did you know that 'full without' means 'completely naked' in Tamil even though 'full' and 'without' are English words?

S: So this is still going on I see.

K: I have decided to write a song about substance abuse and addiction, now that I have experienced it firsthand.

S: What did they look like?

K: Who?

S: The drugs.

K: Bro, it was a two-bit room in the back of nowhere, slow blues playing outside, the air was thick with smoke and whiskey, and on the table was all the drugs man.

S: What drugs?

K: The kind that make you see heaven and steal your soul, man. They were just… piled high.

S: Just a big ole pile of crunchy drugs.

K: The drugs made me see the light bro. But I also saw the… darkness.

S: You sound like a fucking moron.

K: You're just saying that because I'm a brown lady. If I was a white dude everyone would say I was amazing.

S: I'm going to tell Rashmi that you referred to her three-crore luxury apartment as a two-bit room.

K: THE PAIN IS SO BAAAAAD BABY, I NEED THE DRUGS RIGHT NOW. SO GO AND GET THEM FOR ME PLEASE

* * *

K: I just noticed something.

S: Yes?

K: There's these birds in the birdbath.

S: And?

K: And they are all full without.

S: They're birds. They're allowed to be full without.

K: But I think there are ladies birds and gents birds bathing together. I feel like I should do something. For Indian culture.

S: How can you tell which are the ladies and which are the gents?

K: Oh these FUCKING DRUGS! They're messing with my head!

S: Ya no your head is like that only. Naturally.

K: God I hate birds.

* * *

K: I thought you should know that a lot of cartoon characters are in half full without. For example, Donald Duck has a shirt and a cap but no pants.

S: So here's something interesting though—

K: Mickey Mouse wears gloves and shorts but no shirt. I wonder if Donald Duck is the cartoon embodiment of the Real Indian Woman. Because a Real Indian Woman would never wear pants, right?

S: It was herbal cigarettes.

K: What?

S: Remember how you became a drug addict about an hour ago because you sat next to someone with weed? So that wasn't weed, it was herbal cigarettes.

K: It was that dank man, the herb. The wacky tobaccy. The marijuana... banahna.

S: It was herbal cigarettes. Like, with mooligais and all. For asthma and sinus conditions.

K: So there was a little drugs in it then.

S: I'm impressed that you kept this up this long though. Commitment my dude.

K: Well if it wasn't drugs then why was I like that?

S: Because that's just how you are bro. That's just how you are.

Big Kids

K: Hey peanut, what are you doing inside?

N: Nothing.

K: I thought you were down playing with the other kids.

N: I came up.

K: I see that. What happened?

N: They said I'm too small to play.

K: Aw. That sucks.

N: Amma said you're not allowed to say that to me.

K: You want to hang out with your old aunt for a while?

N: No.

K: Help me write this story.

N: I'm too small.

K: Come on, you're weird, this story is weird, it's a winning combination. Anyway, I can see you have some ideas in your head.

N: Where.

K: Right there, behind your ear, I can see.

N: You're just making pretend.

K: Come on, let's start. Once upon a time, there was a…?

N: No.

K: There was a No. And she had a yellow house and purple boots.

N: And a shoe rack.

K: What is it with you and shoe racks?

N: I like shoe racks.

K: OK, then what happened?

N: Nothing.

K: Aw come on, we're just getting started. There was the No, with her yellow house, purple boots and shoe rack. And she found a giant orange in her bathroom.

N: Why come you always say things like that?

K: Like what?

N: Like giant orange in the bathroom.

K: And what would you do if you found a giant orange in your bathroom?

N: Nothing.

K: Nothing. You'd just sit there with a giant orange in your bathroom.

N: Ya.

K: Well you know what No did?

N: What?

K: I have no idea.

N: Hm?

K: I don't know what happened.

N: Maybe No peels the orange.

K: Is the orange alive? Because this will be a very different kind of story if the orange is being peeled alive.

N: You mean does he have eyes and mouth?

K: Yes, exactly.

N: Ya.

K: OK, maybe she doesn't peel him then. Do they become friends?

N: No.

K: Ah, gritty realism. Why not though?

N: Because he ate all her bones. And drank all her blood.

K: Dude! Why?

N: Because he… he was a dentist.

K: Wow, OK.

N: I'm going down again.

K: Really? You don't want to finish this worrying piece of fiction with me?

N: No.

K: OK, have fun. Don't eat anyone.

N: OK.

* * *

K: So! You're back I see.

N: Ya.

K: What happened?

N: Nothing.

K: Big kids still playing?

N: Ya.

K: Want to finish the story?

N: No.

K: Want to draw a picture of a monster eating your house?

N: No.

K: Want to buy some bitcoin?

N: Hm?

K: Should I tell you a story about how when I was little the big kids didn't let me play with them either?

N: No.

K: OK. But you know what I did though?

N: You told your Amma to make them play with you?

K: No, I threw water at them and told them it was pee.

N: Really?

K: You don't do that though. Especially not with real pee. And don't tell anyone I told you that.

N: No one wants to play with me.

K: Aw, I want to play with you. Kind of.

N: I don't have any friends to play with me but.

K: So you're saying I'm not your friend.

N: You're too big.

K: Yeah? Well you're a banana butt.

N: Someone's at the door.

K: Well go see who it is.

N: Amma said you're supposed to answer the door.

K: It's fine, you're better at opening the door than I am.

* * *

K: So let me get this straight, that was one of the big kids and they want you to play with them now because they're playing house and they need a baby.

N: Ya.

K: And did you pooh-pooh them?

N: Hm?

K: Did you pooh-pooh them and say Fie! Away with you and your ageist ways!

N: I'm going down.

K: You're not going to resist? Fight the power? Defeat the… thingy?

N: No, I want to be the baby.

K: What does this say about your generation?

N: I'm going bye.

K: Wow, OK.

N: Don't come down.

K: Oh my God, I wasn't going to come down anyway. Banana butt.

niira radia and the telephone

Once upon a time, there lived a corporate lobbyist named Niira Radia. Like many people, she enjoyed talking on the telephone with her friends. One day, these phone conversations were shared with the rest of the world. How did this happen? Some naughty little pixie must have put a spell on the magical telephone lines! Lo and behold! It was discovered that Niira Radia was using her own magic powers to influence the allocation of certain important ministries in the Kingdom of the Government of India. Two of her telephone friends were from the media and should have told a grown-up, but they didn't. Because of all this topsy-turviness, a terrible thing called The 2G Scam was unearthed, right there in the Kingdom of the Government of India. The townspeople said hey! You can't do that! So Niira Radia decided not to be a corporate lobbyist anymore. And that's basically all that happened.

The End

Lobbying with Niira Radia!!! Wow!!!

K: ohai!

Niira: Hi Vir. Where are you Delhi or…*

K: Hai Vir!!! Is that what we're calling each other now? It's weird but whatever! Anyway, I just got back from the dentist and I feel FAAAANTASTIC! I'm actually in a great deal of pain as well? But it's FAAAAANTASTIC! It's really not though but I'm trying to be positive today. Anyway before we get started just wanted to clarify, I know who you are, right? Like, I'm talking on the phone with someone I know, right?

Niira: Okay. I just wanted to, I've been talking to my Tamil Nadu friends.

K: Seriously why would you start this conversation by showing off that you have Tamil Nadu friends WHEN I HAVE NOBODY!!

Niira: I just need to, I don't know whether you are in the position to get through to anyone at Congress. I just met Kani just now.

K: STOP SHOWING OFF THAT YOU MEET PEOPLE!! AND I CAN TOTALLY GET THROUGH TO ANYONE AT CONGRESS YOU DON'T KNOW MY LIFE. What exactly do you mean by Congress though?

Niira: And I've been, you know, we reunited since yesterday. The problem is…

K: We reunited? As in you and me? Is that a good thing? Or would it have been better if we had stayed apart because it hurts too much when we are together?

---

* Niira Radia's lines are reproduced faithfully from the published transcripts.

Niira: No, I'll tell you what—they are not understanding that they are actually communicating with the wrong guy. Not because I detached Maran but actually the father has not nominated Maran to negotiate. Now, you know, it's like a banana republic where the cabinet…

K: I mean I can really relate with that, I've certainly had my fair share of communicating with the wrong guy. Did you say you detached Maran from a banana cabinet?

Niira: No. He is not, he is not. I know, no. But the Congress is under the impression. They have already apparently indicated to Maran that the Prime Minister will not give infrastructure berth to DMK, which, but he himself is desperately pushing for an infrastructure berth for himself.

K: Right. And we are talking about… train berths now? For some reason? Also, can I just share something with you? Once we had rat problem and the cockyfucker went and died inside the house. ON PURPOSE. And it smelled like anything. I think the best solution is to get those blue biscuit things and make sure the rat eats them and you don't eat them also. That's the really tricky part. But nobody tells you that.

Niira: But the problem is that there is a leader which is Kani's brother which is Azhagiri, who's won that election and he is a mass leader.

K: So interesting because when I was in school, we had assistant class leaders, which got shortened into ass class leaders. This is kind of like mass leaders but not really.

Niira: Now what has apparently Maran has gone and indicated to Congress is that he will accept a MOS independent and you leave it with me, everything will be okay.

K: Also in college, they had student assistant secretaries and they were known as ass secs, which is much worse than ass class because Indian culture. There would be announcements saying all girls please attend the ass secs meeting and then the girls would get in trouble for not going for ass secs meetings. Also no one really listened to these girls either so the population as a whole would get in trouble for not taking ass secs seriously. This is not to be confused with AISEC meetings, which sometimes people called I Suck meetings.

Niira: Which blames Balu, Raja and Maran Cabinet posts independent to Azhagiri and MOS to Kani.

K: So just want to put this out there, I absolutely did not blame anyone. And I don't know what they were blamed for. And I don't know who these people are, especially MOS. Is that like an American name? A WHOLE NEW WORLD, WITH NEW HORIZONS TO PURSUE...

Niira: Now, Azhagiri is a very, you know, he is, he is a mass leader. He controls half of Tamil Nadu for Karunanidhi's point of view.

K: Speaking of hands! You know who has nice hands? Karu Uncle! If you look at some of his pictures, you'll notice his hands are very nice or at least they look nice sometimes in some pictures. Which is heartening, no? To think that you can be this old dude with sunglasses but nice hands are still possible for you. I like to know that's possible.

Niira: He is far too, too senior for Maran. So, what he has told his father that if you make Maran a cabinet minister...

K: This is the banana cabinet... minister?

Niira: ...I'll not come into the cabinet. And the father cannot afford to upset him because...

K: I totally get that, yes. I mean I wouldn't get into a cabinet either, even if it did have bananas in it.

Niira: ...simply because of his position.

K: Exactly. I mean, what can that position even be, right? You have your cabinet, your bananas. I mean it's going to be uncomfortable if nothing else.

Niira: Right now the Congress doesn't seem to be understanding this.

K: That's too bad. Have you thought about diagrams? Show them cabinet this size, bananas this size, so on, so forth. Diagrams always help me when I don't understand something. Actually that's a lie, diagrams never help me. Diagrams are the worst.

Niira: They need to, look, they need to talk directly to Karunanidhi, they need to talk to Kani.

K: This makes a lot of sense because I have always thought that if you need to talk to someone directly, the best way to do that is to talk to someone else. Also, Kani means fruit and banana is a fruit so she is the natural choice for intermediary fruit discussion purposes. Is she planning on speaking to the bananas directly? Is there like a head banana?

Niira: No, she didn't speak to him. Only Prime Minister spoke even that was Kani was translating for him. It was very brief that, you know let's try and resolve this issue. There is nothing at all and whatever. They need to get Ghulam Nabi Azad to speak to Kanimozhi.

K: The bananas need to get Ghulam Nabi Azad to speak to Kanimozhi, okay. I don't have to do anything about this, do I? Because I wouldn't even know how to set something like that up, you know? I mean the procurement of bananas alone would—

Niira: Seriously, that's the only thing that will work and Kani will take them to her father.

K: I see. Well I don't think that should be a problem, as long as Karu Uncle understands that the bananas are not there for eating. Does he even eat bananas though? Because I personally have never seen him eat a banana. Like not even once.

Niira: No. But they need to speak to Kani and Kani will take him to their, her father directly.

K: OK. Well take them in a fruit basket. I have one you can use. Actually it's an old bucket but you can use it anyway. Is there any problem with the cabinet? Because I have another old bucket you can use if there is cabinet problem. I mean what is a cabinet anyway! It's a bucket! With a lid. And hinges. I don't have any hinges.

Niira: He has no problem with three cabinet berths at all. In fact it is the Congress that messed it up.

K: No problem, this bucket can also be used in place of the Congress. It's a multipurpose bucket. It has no handle also.

Niira: Had they, had they not kept on insisting and kept on pushing Maran forward themselves have been pushing Maran forward. They would have left it to Raja and, and Balu even if they wanted or Raja and Azhagiri and Kani would taken independent, nobody will, it is Congress they started this whole Maran dialogue.

K: Well, I think we can agree on one thing. All of them are not going to fit in the cabinet. Especially if the bananas are already in there. Yes. Yes. Yes. Yes.

Niira: No. No. No. No, they did, they've sent a list earlier with five portfolios and Maran's name because father was pushed… so he had to send a list with everybody's name on it. But he was hoping that Congress would come back and say okay we will accept Raja or we will not, or not Raja, we will give you only three portfolios right? But they have not able to, the communication that's been happening in Congress with DMK has been complete warped. They are talking to the wrong guys.

K: I mean it's just so clear to me right now that in this whole situation, the bananas are the most powerful entities at the moment and the only ones who know what is going on. After all, they are occupying the cabinet, no?

Niira: The, the simplest way is Kani [Indiscernible] [0:03:24].

K: Naturally, you need to exploit that fruit connection as much as you can. You can call it the Tutti Frutti Talks.

Niira: And Kani [Indiscernible] [0:03:27] will take them to her father directly.

K: Right. But make sure you're prepared for any and all eventualities. Primarily, don't eat the bananas. But if he does, then what will you have? Banana peels. Cows like banana peels. Putting cows inside cabinets, very difficult.

Niira: And they can have this, you know, whatever are the, the concerns, whatever they want to say, let them say in front of Kani.

K: You know what I think? I think right now that as bananas, their major concerns would be that they don't get eaten by anyone.

Niira: Yeah, they should say, they should say we don't want Maran.

K: They should say we don't want Maran or anyone eating us because that's mean and we would die.

Niira: But the moment you drop Maran, your problem gets resolved because Azhagiri has done okay.

K: I'm sure the bananas don't want Azhagiri to eat them either. That's just my opinion though.

Niira: Yeah.

K: Listen, why don't you do one thing. Change your last name to Radio. Then your name will be Niira Radio, like Near A Radio and that would be neat. Why don't you just try it out now?

Niira: Okay. Give him this message. She is right now…

K: …Near A Radio. See? Do you see what I'm saying? It would be so useful for your name to also pinpoint your location also. Like a GPS name. So like if someone says who is that lady and where is she, I can say Near A Radio and that's neat for all people involved. I think maybe you'd have to make sure you were near a radio at all times but whatever. Why don't you try again?

Niira: [Indiscernible] [0:03:51] She is in her South Avenue residence.

K: Ah, see? That sounds boring. So instead, you can say She is Near A Radio instead, because that's interesting even if it's not necessarily true. Try again.

Niira: I just met her.

K: I just met Near A Radio. See? Isn't that neat? Again, go again.

Niira: And some Tamil Nadu Congress guys also want just now to meet her.

K: Some Tamil Nadu Congress guys also want just now to meet Near A Radio. I think you're getting the hang of this. Keep practicing and you can get PhD in this or something.

Niira: I don't think it needs to be done at that level. It needs to be done at, at Ghulam Nabi Azad level or...

K: OK, PhD don't want, you try for Ghulam Nabi Azad level or whatever ranking systems they are having. And don't forget to change your last name to Radio.

Niira: Yeah.

K: Awesome. We do know each other though, right? Right?

an indifferent history of the kingdom of facebook

Once upon a time, Facebook was a shimmering, sugary blister, encouraging people to poke each other, while shyly hiding the fact that it was letting a naughty little consulting firm called Cambridge Analytica collect user data without their consent. During that time, many brave and valiant users used their Facebook powers to battle the many social evils of their time. They battled natural disasters by changing their display pictures, and met each tragedy head on with thoughts, prayers, and heartfelt words about how said tragedy was upsetting them so much you guys. They did all this and nothing happened.

The End

Let's Change the World with Facebook!!!

S: What did I do today? I sat on the floor for a while. I sat on a chair. It was a lot.

K: I did a lot of charity work today. Like, a LOT.

S: And when you say charity, do you mean you absolutely did not do charity?

K: I've done charity! That one time.

S: Giving something to someone by accident and forgetting to get it back is not charity my dude.

K: What about when I gave away my clothes.

S: Are you talking about that box of stuff that you kept forgetting to throw away and was sitting in your place for so long it was being used as a side table?

K: There may have been a box.

S: Dude, giving your garbage to someone is not charity, that is garbage disposal.

K: Why do you hate India so much bro?

S: I don't think you even know what charity is.

K: I DO SO!! For instance, today I joined a Facebook group called STOP POVERTY RIGHT NOW I MEAN IT YOU GUYS!!!!!

S: And that is charity because...

K: Because we're not fooling around, ok? This group is based in London. So you know it's serious because it probably has white people. Or people who know white people.

S: Do they have poverty in London? Or is that just an India and Her Multicolour Friends thing?

K: Maybe they don't have poverty anymore because of the Facebook page.

S: I like this idea.

K: So anyway, being an Online Soldier for Poverty—

S: I'm sorry, a what?

K: An Online Soldier for Poverty.

S: You're a soldier *for* poverty? As in imma get everyone some poverty?

K: No no. Although I can see how you might think that.

S: You guys are fighting for poverty for everyone.

K: No! Wait, are we?

S: What exactly are your duties as a soldier?

K: Well today I put up status updates to raise awareness about famine in Africa—

S: Which country?

K: What?

S: Which country in Africa?

K: What?

S: Wow dude.

K: Yeah so to raise awareness about famine in Africa and endangered animals in America.

S: Why can't you save endangered animals in India?

K: Not 'save', *raise awareness*. Awareness is more important.

S: Okay, why can't you raise awareness about endangered animals in India?

K: Well if they don't have a Facebook page, then how can I?

S: Okay wait, what exactly happens when you Facebook about endangered marmosets or whatever?

K: I think someone gets a quarter?

S: Who gets a quarter?

K: What?

S: Are you giving them this quarter?

K: Fuck no.

S: Then who is giving the quarter?

K: I'm sure someone has this information.

S: Some dude is giving a quarter and some other dude is taking a quarter.

K: Yes.

S: And this is the charity.

K: So they tell me. Oh! And I played this video game for charity! It had this malnourished brown kid and you had to find food to feed it before it starved to death! I can't remember what it was for though. I want to say… improvement of sports facilities? Maybe?

S: Maybe it was a charity video game for India! Like India in general.

K: Hey! Then they could give *me* money! Because I live in India!

S: Yes. Because that's how that works.

K: This is absolutely going to happen to me.

S: What else did you do, besides all this amazing charity work?

K: I had a nap. I ate some Horlicks. I had a nap.

S: Posting status updates is the charity work you did today.

K: Yes.

S: You are a fucking moron.

K: I did not realize charity was so hard bro.

S: A. FUCKING. MORON.

K: I shall have another nap to recuperate.

the magical kingdom of jersey shore

Once upon a time, in a far away land called New Jersey, there lived a reality TV show called Jersey Shore. In that show, there lived a young person named Snooki. Snooki had many adventures with her friends and these adventures were shared with everyone on the television box. Sometimes people liked Snooki! Sometimes people did not like Snooki. People took to the internet to write all about their many Snooki feelings. And they had many, many, many feelings. Even privileged people in exotic India wrote about Snooki. They wrote about Snooki even though terribly important things were happening in their own country. They wrote about Snooki even though they weren't completely sure what a Jersey Shore was. Such was the power of Snooki. One day, the magical kingdom of Jersey Shore disappeared. Snooki went to Celebrity Land and lived there with all her money. And all those many, many Snooki internet feelings were soon buried under so many other internet feelings about so many other things.

The End

I Bet You Don't Remember Who Snooki Is Cos I Sure Don't!!!

K: You know what I hate about Indian TV? There's nothing to watch. Like, nothing.

S: Unless you're still living in the socialist Doordarshan era, there's about 900 channels to watch now.

K: There's no Jersey Shore. I want to watch Jersey Shore.

S: Why?

K: There's someone called Snooki on it and she got punched by some guy.

S: Snooki is a person?

K: Yeah, she's Snooki. She got punched by some guy.

S: Where is Jersey anyway, is it in Chicago? Is it where mobsters come from?

K: I feel like it's in Canada? Anyway, I just want to see what all the fuss is about with Snooki. And The Situation.

S: What situation?

K: The Situation is this guy but he's not the guy that punched Snooki. The Situation used to be an exotic dancer which I think means he used to be a stripper.

S: Do you have videos of him stripping?

K: No.

S: Then why are we even talking about this?

K: Snooki said she would change the world by installing a tanning bed in every home.

S: Yeah I don't care about this anymore.

* * *

K: Oh my God, I just had the weirdest dream!

S: Remember how we decided you wouldn't tell me your dreams anymore because your subconscious is very disturbing and also because I don't care?

K: I dreamed about Snooki! Only she looked like Sridevi from the Hawa Hawaii song and these tubelights were beating her up with tanning beds and shouting Snooki! Theerpu maathi sollu!

S: Eh?

K: I think that happened because I watched *Nattamai* before falling asleep.

S: I miss Hawa Hawaii Sridevi. I miss that Bollywood. What happened to it? Where did it go?

K: Eye see you see something something Mombaasa ping pong.

S: You know what song I really miss? Tama Tama Loge.

K: Tu Premi.

S: A-ha!

K: Mein Premi.

S: A-ha!

K: Tu Raazi.

S: OK, enough.

K: Hey, did I tell you I found this Jersey Shore Nickname Generator online? Guess what my Jersey Shore name is. Guess guess.

S: Bro, I must vehemently reiterate. I am not interested in your dreams, or this New Jersey… River?

K: JERSEY SHORE

S: Or Snooker or whatever her name is.

K: Pookie.

S: I don't think it was Pookie. It's close though.

K: No my Jersey Shore name is Pookie.

S: And what are we to make of this.

K: That the Jersey Shore Nickname Generator was not designed for Indian names.

S: Fucking racists.

K: I HATE RACISM SO MUCH OH MY GOD

baby twitter and the kashmir adventure

Once upon a time, when Twitter was still a baby and everyone was mostly on Facebook, there came news of unrest in Kashmir. In order to prove their patriotism and that the caps lock was functioning on their keyboard, many fine people took to endlessly tweeting things like KASHMIR BELONGS TO INDIA and KASHMIR IS OURS and KASHMIR DOES NOT BELONG TO PAKISTAN BECAUSE IT BELONGS TO INDIA OK. Many attempts at a nuanced or even just an informed discussion were quickly nipped in the bud because JAI HIND. People all over Indian Twitter Land were either 'educating' people on Kashmir, telling people to get educated on Kashmir, or telling everyone what Kashmiris want and what was best for Kashmir. All this was done with little to no knowledge about Kashmir at all because lol why would anyone do that tho. Baby Twitter soon grew into whatever it is today, and was bought by a man who wants to colonize Mars. We are still not allowed to say anything about Kashmir though because as always JAI HIND

The End

Kashmir Beautiful Kashmir

S: I've heard that phrase a lot though. 'It smelled as bad as day-old Indian food.' Seems to be a popular way of describing very bad smells in America. I mean it makes you wonder what they're putting in the 'Indian food' over there, no?

K: Right.

S: Because day-old Indian food isn't supposed to smell like a dirty diaper. But for some reason, that's what it smells like in America!

K: Also, what does this say about us who live in India and often eat day-old food and don't think it smells bad?

S: It means we eat gross things. They should have a Discovery program about us called 'Ew Gross! Indians Who Eat Day Old Indian Food In India!' With a nice white host who makes faces into the camera and describes in a historical, cultural and geographic context how gross we are.

K: I would absolutely not watch that. At all.

S: Anyway, as I was saying, my international guests.

K: Oh right! From South Africa wow so exotic.

S: You know anything about South Africa? Apart from the fact that they have a cricket team? And it's in the south of Africa?

K: So I think the way it goes is, South Africans are cool unless they are white, in which case they are racist because apartheid.

S: My guests are white.

K: Okay. So they are racists then.

S: I'm actually leaning more towards 'Just because they are white and from South Africa does not mean they are racist.'

K: Yeah but I saw this documentary and all the white South Africans were racists and white supremacists. Like ALL of them. Everyone they talked to was like totally into racism and white power and whatever.

S: What kind of documentary was this?

K: It was about white supremacists in South Africa.

S: Why do I even talk to you?

K: It was a very classy documentary! The person doing the voice-over had a British accent! And also I watched that movie with Leonardo DiCaprio and he was also racist and South African and he called everyone bru. Like the coffee. Ithu Bru Ma!

S: I think it's cool how you clearly don't know anything about this but you're going on talking like you do.

K: Also, I believe it's customary to welcome white South Africans with some kind of choir-like song because that's what happened in *The Gods Must Be Crazy*. You have to wear bright colours and wave your hands in a non-threatening manner.

S: Cool. Okay before I hang up on you, one number question. I'm doing an informal poll-type thing. What do you know about Kashmir?

K: KASHMIR BEAUTIFUL KASHMIR

S: Oh my God.

K: KASHMIR WONDERFUL KASHMIR

S: And that's all you know about Kashmir.

K: Also fightingfighting.

S: You know why fightingfighting?

K: Because they are angry? About something?

S: You think maybe India has someth—

K: YOU FUCKING ANTI-PATRIOTIC FUCKING PAKISTANI FUCKING FUCKING FUCKER! HOW DARE YOU SAY ANYTHING BAD ABOUT INDIA!

S: I jus—

K: KASHMIR BELONGS TO INDIA, YOU ANTI-PATRIOTIC ASSHOLE!

S: The people who live there—

K: WHO THE FUCK CARES ABOUT THE PEOPLE WHO LIVE THERE? KASHMIR BELONGS TO INDIA, YOU FUCKING PAKISTANI!

S: Okay.

K: JAI HIND!!! YOU DACOITY GOONDA NAXALITE MAOIST FEMINIST!!!

S: Okay.

K: KASHMIR

S: Okay.

K: BEAUTIFUL KASHMIR

S: Right.

* * *

Indian Weltanschauung*: What South African culture? South Africans have no culture! They are all rogues and rapists. They are like Australians only they live in Africa!

S: Right. I just thought since you lived there for a while maybe you knew some—

Indian Weltanschauung: I only socialized with Indians. From India. The Indians in South Africa are as bad as the whites. All loose women.

S: Okay.

Indian Weltanschauung: See, I know too well about white South Africans. And what I can say is that all white South Africans are rogues and rapists.

* wtf is a weltanschauung??

S: But you never actually interacted with them.

Indian Weltanschauung: I never interact with such people. Rogues and rapists.

S: Didn't you say the exact same thing about Americans?

Indian Weltanschauung: I know too well about Americans. Rogues and rapists.

S: And you know this because you lived in America for a while but you never interacted with Americans because you only hung out with Indians from India because the Indian-Americans were as bad as the whites, especially the loose women.

Indian Weltanschauung: Exactly.

S: You say that about all countries, no? Except India, of course.

Indian Weltanschauung: I'm very well-traveled. I often go to new countries, experience new cultures and meet new people.

S: That is awesome. One more thing, just a random question. What do you know about Kashmir?

Indian Weltanschauung: I know too well about Kashmiris. All rogues and rapists.

S: So you know about the fighting there.

Indian Weltanschauung: Big blow to India's film industry. Basically it's because all Kashmiris only know how to throw stones. Take it from me. I know them too well.

S: You think maybe India has something to do with the fighti—

Indian Weltanschauung: How dare you say such things?! India is great!

S: But—

Indian Weltanschauung: India is great!

S: But there's—

Indian Weltanschauung: India is great!

S: But some—

Indian Weltanschauung: India is great India is great India is great!

S: Okay.

Indian Weltanschauung: I think maybe you are getting confused about all this, better you stop reading so much feminist propaganda.

S: Awesome I will do that.

* * *

SexehBewbies: DIE ANTWOORD!!

S: Eh?

SexehBewbies: South African hip hop.

S: And this is all you know about South Africa?

SexehBewbies: What's cool though is that I think they rap in their South African language or whatever so if I'm playing it and someone asks 'What are they saying?' then I go 'South African hip hop, bru' and they go like 'Ohhh' like they know I'm the man because I listen to South African hip hop. You know?

S: Maybe they're rapping in Afrikaans.

SexehBewbies: Well yeah, obviously they are rapping Africans, I mean South Africa is in Africa, so yes, they are going to be rapping Africans. Also as a feminist, I feel like I do need to mention that one of their songs sounded kind of rapey but it's hard to tell if they were just being ironic or South African.

S: The Indian Weltanschauung told me all white South Africans are rogues and rapists.

SexehBewbies: The Indian Weltanschauung told me all Indians who drink Rooh Afza are Pakistani spies.

S: Not rogues and rapists?

SexehBewbies: Rogues and rapists also. But mainly Pakistani spies. Hey, can I come and say hi to your South Africans? I can talk to them about Die Antwoord. Because if they are South African and white then they HAVE to like Die Antwoord and it will make them feel safe and at home to talk to a nice public Indian fellow who knows about Die Antwoord.

S: This could be like how you kept talking to those German people about Rammstein. Even though they kept telling you that they didn't like Rammstein.

SexehBewbies: How can you be German and not like Rammstein? That's like being Japanese and not liking Dir En Grey.

S: One question I wanted to ask.

SexehBewbies: AskAsk.

S: What do you know about Kashmir?

SexehBewbies: I really don't like Kashmir apples.

S: There's also like that whole fightingfighting thing happening there also, no? Remember?

SexehBewbies: Oh right! Yeah, that too. War is bad, man.

S: You think maybe India has someth—

SexehBewbies: Whoa, whoa, no need to get all Che Guevara there! What's with the fascism?

S: Eh?

SexehBewbies: You're getting all anarchist and anti-India and stuff and it's not cool.

S: But I didn't even—

SexehBewbies: Stop it dude, you're being gross! India is totally justified in doing whatever it's doing up there. Don't be all weird and Marxist and shit. It's so fucking creepy when people get all Maoist and whatever.

S: You don't know what's happening in Kashmir do you.

SexehBewbies: No. But I do know that India is awesome. I really don't like those apples though.

* * *

K: But why???

S: Well between you, Indian Weltanschauung insisting on coming over to protect me from the raping white South Africans, and SexehBewbies insisting on coming over to talk to them about Die Antwoord, I thought maybe better if I just met them somewhere you guys can't find us. Especially since there are going to be some Kashmiris there also.

K: Oh nice. You're hanging out with white supremacists and anti-India militants. Real patriotic. If I tweet about this, you'll be in big trouble. People will call you names and they'll do it in allcaps with lots of exclamation marks. And if we're really pissed off, we'll demand you get booked for sedation, seduction and Sadducees.

S: Look, if it makes you feel better, I'm sorry, the white South Africans are sorry for being white South Africans and the Kashmiris are sorry for being Kashmiris. In fact we're all sorry for everything.

K: Whatever. Oh, I forgot to tell you. South Africans are into boars.

S: You think you're saying Boer don't you?

K: Is that not the South African word for boar?

S: No.

K: South Africa is complicated.

S: At least it's not as complicated as Kashmir.

K: Yeah. India is awesome. Jai Hind, man.

S: Jai Hind.

All the British characters are honest, jolly souls while all the "natives" are scheming, treacherous, unscrupulous devils. All but one!! The solitary exception is Gunga Din, the faithful water-

carrier—loyal unto death, despite the insults and curses that are invariably showered on him by his White Masters. He is always cringing before them. **The word "cringing" occurs innumerable times in the scenario, for that is Gunga Din's consistent pattern of behaviour.** That is how all loyal "natives" must behave in the presence of their rulers!

Mr. S. Satyamurti: In view of the fact that anti-Indian films are more poisonous outside India than inside India, will the Government of India take some steps to see that the India Office does examine these films with these excisions and satisfies itself and satisfies the Government of India that these films, with these excisions, are not anti-Indian?

Who and what was "Gunga Din" that he should be "immortalized" by this picture? Those who are familiar with the works of that greatest of all Imperialist propagandist poets, Rudyard Kipling, will recall a poem by this name.

It is not a long poem and tells the simple story of "Gunga Din", a regimental water-carrier on the North Western Frontier, who dies in an attempt to save the lives of British soldiers who are being attacked by marauding Pathans. The purpose is obvious: to impress the world with the devotion of Indians and to teach the "natives" that the highest ambition in their lives must be such an opportunity to serve their White masters. When

tion.

"Every Indian must put down his head in shame when he realizes that this dirty propaganda against us is being shamelessly broadcast

in other parts of the world and we are unable to stop it.

It began with "India Speaks." Then came, in quick succession, "Lives of a Bengal Lancer", "Clive of India", "Wee Willie Winkie", "Tiger of Eschnapur" and only too recently, "The Drum", the Alexander Korda film which was banned in several Indian provinces and raised a storm of protest all over India due to the excellent lead given by "filmindia." But in none of these films has our country been libelled so grotesquely as in "Gunga Din", the R.K.O. Radio picture which is shortly to be released. It is an Imperialist propaganda of the crudest, the most vulgar sort and depicts Indians as nothing better than sadistic barbarians. It will make the stomach of every Indian—and every fair-minded foreigner—turn with disgust. Some of the scenes in it are revolting, nauseating.

Communalism, Sectarianism. Provincialism. Favouritism—I regard them all as equally pernicious. They all arise from a narrow outlook and stunted imagination. They are all different symptoms of the same disease but, owing to the acute political tension in our country, when anything takes a communal turn it becomes far more dangerous. Then is the time to take drastic action, even if it means the amputation of the diseased limb.

How well these five "experts" know about India is revealed by the same bulletin from which I quote the following:

"And perhaps in the still desert air will come the voice of the "**muezzin**" from the minaret in Tantrapur filling the air with **Hindu** fatalism....What is written is written."

"Minaret", **"Muezzin"** and **"Hindu"** fatalism! What an authentic India!!

the Hon. Sir Reginald Maxwell, Home Member, Government of India, admitted that no Indian was serving on the Committee that sees anti-Indian pictures on behalf of the India Office. Evidently the Englishmen still know what is good for India

This issue of "Filmindia" is dedicated to "Gunga Din" the Poor Indian Bhisti who, as Kipling sings in his famous poem, died like a faithful dog for his white masters and in dying left behind an excuse to the white-men to slander his country and countrymen.

How tragic is that death which bequeathes to the country a heritage of slander and abuse at the hands of the white men of the West?

And yet, let "Gunga Din", the Indian, live in the memory of man for **"he was a better man"** than his white masters.

The Women's University Club of America with its formidable membership of distinguished women of America must be having good reasons to say: **"Gunga Din carries on the tradition of Great Britain's supremacy in India".**

And yet Sir Reginald "thinks" (of course, without seeing) that "Gunga Din" is not offensive to the Indian sentiment. Since when has the Indian sentiment been wedded to the British imperialism?

warren anderson and the naughty leak

Once upon a time, there lived a dude called Warren Anderson. He was the Chair and CEO of the Union Carbide Corporation. In 1984, a naughty leak in the UCC pesticide plant in Bhopal led to what has since been called the worst industrial disaster in the world. The government of Madhya Pradesh paid compensation to the families of 3787 official victims of the Bhopal gas leak, but other sources put the death toll above 16,000. In 2006, a government affidavit stated that the leak 'caused 558,125 injuries including 38,478 temporary partial injuries and approximately 3,900 severely and permanently disabling injuries.' The soil and groundwater continue to be contaminated to this day. It was a very, very, naughty leak indeed! And who was responsible for this naughty, naughty leak? Warren Anderson! Because of all this bothersome bother of people dying and stuff like that, Warren Anderson had to fly all the way to India to be arrested. And India is so very far away! Six hours after he was arrested, he was released on $2,100 bail. Whereupon Warren Anderson tripped prettily onto an airplane and flew all the way back home to America. And he stayed there for three whole years! Then in 1987, the Indian Government said hey! Come back here Warren Anderson! We want to charge you with homicide! But the UCC stuck out its tongue, waggled its bum and said YOU'RE NOT THE BOSS OF ME! In 1992, the Indian Government said hey! Warren! Come back here! And Warren said oh no no! I will not go! In 2003, a formal extradition request was issued and sweetly rejected by the United States. In 2009, the chief judicial magistrate of Bhopal issued a warrant for Warren Anderson's arrest. About a month later, the Union Carbide Corporation said they had no part in all this naughty leaky business because that Union Carbide Corporation plant, which was owned by Union Carbide Corporation, was operated by Union Carbide India Limited, which was also owned by Union Carbide Corporation but also a totally different thing entirely because it was in India. Warren Anderson never had to go to India ever again. He lived happily ever after in America until he died in 2014, at the ripe old age of 92.

The End

Life Is Very Confusing Dears and Kevin

S: You made an actual list.

K: Yes.

S: Aren't you supposed to be job-hunting?

K: I feel like you're being really aggressive with me right now.

S: Why did you feel the need to make a list of all the things you don't understand? And why did you feel like you had to do it today?

K: There's just so much stuff! It's hard to keep track bro. Like Rooh Afza for instance.

S: Can you just stop it with the whole Rooh Afza thing, no one cares.

K: But I don't understand! Why do I keep drinking it? Why??

S: Because you're an idiot.

K: If there's one drink I can't stand it's Rooh Afza. But then I'll go to someone's house, they'll bring me a glass, and it looks so red and sparkly like it's going to taste like artificial strawberries and happiness and then BAM! Rooh Afza.

S: Like I said earlier, no one cares.

K: And then I seriously don't understand why no one is interested in my movie *GhettoDawg BlingBling: The Rise of Kevin*.

S: This is something you don't understand?

K: It's a musical about poor white American children overcoming their poverty and repairing the hole in the ozone layer through disco! I mean COME ON!

S: Doesn't this movie already exist?

K: Not with Kevin it doesn't.

S: Why isn't Kevin called Kumar though? Or Kenakootam?

K: BECAUSE HE'S KEVIN OMG

S: Or Kasmaalam.

K: Anyway, I also don't understand why we're having so much trouble bringing Warren Anderson back. Is he hiding? Should we use Google Earth to find him?

S: I think it's more of a 'I'm not going to India and you can't make me' situation. Which is not really hiding.

K: Imagine if some Indian dude nuked a bunch of Americans and just ran back home and refused to come back and answer for his crimes.

S: Imagine if Kevin did this.

K: STOP MALIGNING KEVIN

S: Do you know when they finally handed out some compensation, it was just $500? Imagine if they had killed all those people in America and said, aw my bad y'all, here's $500.

K: My favourite part was when the spokesperson said '$500 is plenty good for an Indian'. Now, maybe you're thinking, this spokesperson was an asshole from 1827. And you would be wrong, because this spokesperson was an asshole from 2001!

K: We had internet in 2001! Wikipedia was invented in 2001! WHAT THE ACTUAL FUCK YOU GUYS

S: This whole thing gives me cluster headaches. Anyway,

K: Anyway. Moving on from the world's worst industrial disaster. I don't understand why some people keep screaming 'I HATE INTERCASTE MARRIAGE!!!' at me.

S: They're screaming it AT you? Like they walk up to you in the street and say 'I HATE INTERCASTE MARRIAGE!!!'?

K: Yes.

S: Well you have to let them live their truth bro.

K: But am I supposed to be doing something about intercaste marriage? Do they want me to make a sign?

S: I think they are concerned that you might not know how they feel about intercaste marriage.

K: A sign might help.

S: Here's what I think. And it's a little crazy, I know. But I think that if you don't like intercaste marriage, then you shouldn't have an intercaste marriage. It's just my feeling.

K: That is crazy man.

S: I know, right?

K: You're so edgy.

S: I'm a rebel. A true outsider. A misfit. A renegade.

K: When you say all those words I only think of white dudes wearing leather jackets and standing next to motorcycles.

S: I'm sure that from far away, I look like a white dude in a leather jacket standing next to a motorcycle. A very brown white dude lady.

K: Then I don't understand why 'Summer of '69' is such a popular song in my country.

S: Neither do I. That and 'Hotel California'.

K: For some reason, we the privileged urban, English-speaking dudes of India feel these old white dudes are speaking our language. We hear the words 'I got my first real six string, bought it at the five and dime' and we're like, same bro, same.

S: ON A DARK DESERT HIGHWAY, COOL WIND IN MY HAIR

K: BRO I RELATE TO THESE EXPERIENCES!

S: WARM SMELL OF… MY PEACHES?

K: Yaaru?

S: The bleaches?

K: Colitas.

S: Appadina?

K: Nobody knows.

S: SOMEBODY KNOWS

K: The internet says it means marijuana. Or butts.

S: Let's go with butts. Warm smell of butts rising up in the air.

K: Then I don't understand why people say feminism and homosexuality are CIA plots.

S: They are though.

K: I know but—

S: YOU THINK THEY AREN'T???

K: They are, they are!!

S: What better way to weaken a country than to make the women say they don't want to be raped and stuff.

K: And if everyone is gay, how will we have more girl child for the nation?

S: And everyone knows more girl child would lead to more feminism GOD I HATE THE CIA

K: I also want to know why we don't call honour killings 'murder'? Why does that get a special name with two words and all?

S: Because honour killings sounds better. Murder makes it sound like people were killed.

K: Then I don't understand—

S: How many more of these are there?

K: Just a few. Two or three.

S: More than forty?

K: Maybe more that forty. Maybe like… oh, one hundred and sixty-seven, something like that.

S: Nope. Naan jooties.

K: But—

S: Jooties bro.

K: But I just wanted to— Hello? Ah go fuck yourself anyways.

Great White Hope

S: I think she meant 'dusky'. Not 'desky'.

K: Oh.

S: 'Desky complexion' makes no sense. Especially if she was trying to sell you a whitening cream.

K: Yeah, I couldn't figure out if 'desky' was good or bad.

S: Did she say you were pretty BUT dusky? Or did she say you needed to buy whitening cream because if you didn't your head would fall off?

K: She didn't say anything about pretty, she just said I was dusky.

S: Oh.

K: Apparently my duskiness had completely cancelled out whatever prettiness I may have once had.

S: And the only way to make everything better was to buy eleventy-twelvty million rupees worth of whitening cream?

K: Yes. It was a difficult journey, but in the end, I finally understood that I was the most worst human being ever because I was dark. I said, bro! You mean dark like I'm a Dark Lord? And she said no. And she said not to call her bro again.

S: I had no idea that being 'dark' had such far-reaching consequences!

K: It does! Did you know that the reason I can't get married or get a job or generally be successful at anything is because my skin is dark and evil.

S: I thought you couldn't get a job because you weren't looking for one.

K: That's what I thought too. But it's because of my dark and evil skin.

S: Huh. You learn something everyday dontcha.

K: Then I was like, what about global terrorism? Who is killing the rain-forests? Who let the dogs out? I mean, it was probably me, right?

S: Maybe you really are a Dark Lord.

K: So I said, bro! This is terrible! I mean, I don't want my skin colour to cause global warming and make trees commit suicide. And she said I already told you not to call me bro.

S: She did actually.

K: Then she showed me this whitening cream that was like a kajillion rupees. And she said it was for lightening pigmentation, scrubbing off dead skin cells and probably other stuff but the Gopal Pal Podi jingle was running through my head so I wasn't really listening.

S: I fucking love that song dude.

K: Then I realized what this whitening cream was actually going to do. It was going to turn me into a white person. An authentic, I-Love-All-Coloured-People, Indian-Food-Gives-Me-Diarrhea white person.

S: Whaaaaaaaat!

K: This whitening cream would make my desky skin lighter and lighter until—

S: Until you became invisible?

K: Until my brown skin turned white. And a person with white skin is a white person.

S: I don't think it works that way if you were a brown person first.

K: This whiteness could help me achieve the dream of every true and patriotic Indian.

S: You mean moving to America?

K: Yes! As a white person I would probably have a nicer time in places like Arizona.

S: Isn't Arizona in Brazil or something?

K: Eh?

S: Arizona? Big river with a bunch of trees?

K: That's the Amazon.

S: OK. And that's something different that's not Arizona.

K: The Amazon is not Arizona.

S: OK. The 'A's and 'Z's confused me.

K: Anyway, then I wanted to know if there were different kinds of whitening cream, like to become Russian-White or Italian-White.

S: So that sounds racist but there are no Russian or Italian people here so I guess it's OK.

K: Then she wanted me to leave.

S: Aw. Maybe she was Italian or something.

K: I am doomed to be a Desky Dark Lord forever. Forests will die and children will become serial killers because of me.

S: Bummer you can't be white and go to America now.

K: I COULD HAVE BROUGHT BACK WARREN ANDERSON!!

The Yellow Leddies Coalition Committee Organization Meeting

S: The good news is that The Yellow Leddies Coalition Committee Organization meeting will be held as scheduled.

K: Yay alcohol!

S: Now about the alcohol,

K: Yay!

S: One of our Yellow Leddies just had jaundice, as you know.

K: Yes, she was a literal Yellow Leddies.

S: So she can't have any alcohol because she might die or something.

K: That's so weird!

S: Ya so anyway, we thought that as a sign of solidarity, we would not have any alcohol at this Yellow Leddies Coalition Committee Organization meeting.

K: I don't understand.

S: We're not having any alcohol.

K: What are you saying?

S: Anyway, we must have some other form of entertainments instead of alcohol.

K: How about Uno?

S: You want to substitute alcohol with Uno?

K: Oh! How about an exotic dancer? I know one called SexehBewbies.

S: How does your brain go from Uno to exotic dancers called SexehBewbies?

K: SexehBewbies likes playing Uno.

S: Is that part of her act?

K: SexehBewbies is a dude.

S: Oh! Like a drag queen?

K: No, he's a very generic kind of dude who likes to lift his shirt up and show off his bewbies when he's dancing.

S: You think our Yellow Leddies would be appreciating exotic male dancer called SexehBewbies?

K: Probably not as much as the alcohol. But whattodo.

S: You ask and tell, ah?

K: He will say yes only. He is a very public fellow.

* * *

K: But I said you were exotic male dancer.

SexehBewbies: So?

K: Dancing to Dandanakka Sarukku is not exotic.

SexehBewbies: Ya but I like lifting my shirt to that song and anyway I can do whatever I want.

K: I'm not sure if that qualifies as dancing though.

SexehBewbies: You get to see my tits! What more do you want?

K: Can you juggle or something? Hang on, one another call is coming.

* * *

S: One of our Yellow Leddies has sent me a message asking 'Will he be exposing?'

K: Exposing what?

S: I don't know.

K: Like investigative journalism?

S: Wait, I'll ask.

* * *

S: So apparently not exposing like investigative journalism. Exposing like exposing peanuts.

K: Exposing peanuts?

S: That's what she texted, 'Will he be exposing peanuts?'

K: I don't know if he has any peanuts. Hang on, I'll ask.

* * *

SexehBewbies: I guess I could buy some. What do you want me to do with them?

K: Maybe eat them in an exotic way? Like with a knife and fork or something? Or chopsticks?

SexehBewbies: Or I could throw them around I guess. In an exotic manner.

K: You could do that.

SexehBewbies: I better go get some and start practicing. I've never danced with peanuts before!

* * *

S: About that peanuts thing.

K: He's just gone to get some.

S: Apparently the question was 'will he be exposing penis'.

K: How did 'penis' become 'peanuts'?

S: Slight confusions happened because this Yellow Leddies likes to spell it 'peanus'. Which I like very much actually.

K: Oh my God me too!

S: So will he?

K: Lemme ask.

* * *

SexehBewbies: But I bought all these peanuts!

K: Does this mean no?

SexehBewbies: My house is filled with peanuts! What am I going to do with all these fucking peanuts?!

K: I can understand if you want to say no. Although I think you should do it because guys like showing people their penises. Penii. Penium.

SexehBewbies: I can't find my fucking bathroom chappals because they're somewhere under all these fucking bags of fucking peanuts!

K: Okay, Imma just tell them no because I have a feeling this means no.

* * *

K: Are you guys sure you don't want peanuts instead? Because peanuts can totally happen right now. Peanuts abundance is happening.

S: Here's the thing. A number of Yellow Leddies are saying forget exotic male dancer and just do alcohol for the meeting.

K: What about solidarity for jaundicecase?

S: Solidarity don't want.

K: But SexehBewbies bought all these peanuts.

S: How much? So much?

K: SO much.

S: Okay, hang on.

* * *

K: So the bad news is that you can't show us your penis.

SexehBewbies: I wasn't going to show you my penis.

K: You wanted to.

SexehBewbies: No.

K: DON'T LIE! Anyway, it has been decided that you will be made an honorary Yellow Leddies for your trouble.

SexehBewbies: No thanks. You guys made me super uncomfortable.

K: You mean you feel bad you couldn't show us your dick.

S: Dude, it is all kinds of fucked up for you to think I want to show you my penis just because I have one.

K: Really? If I had a penis I would show it to everyone all the time. I would literally be running in the streets going SEE MUH PENIS!

S: Has anyone ever told you that you are super problematic?

K: Has anyone ever told you that you talk like a girl? Because you do.

WISH YOU
SUCCESS IN
FUTURE
ENDEVOURS

A Cyclone and a Flood

S: Someone told me that cyclones are like the common cold.

K: Like there is no cure for them.

S: Like they keep coming back. A cyclone is not going to say, Oh, I came here already, I guess I'll go hit Bangladesh instead.

K: Cyclones always hit Bangladesh.

S: Can you can see the sun?

* * *

K: The sun is gone. Electricity's gone. And I found these incense sticks that smell like marijuana.

S: All coastal areas are being evacuated.

K: What do they do with evacuated people?

S: Put them in government schools.

K: I saw this show once where pedophiles kept disguising themselves as schools. They showed these kids walking home but the school was following them and nobody noticed because it was a school. I thought it was funny, is that bad?

S: How much incense do you have going there?

K: Lots.

* * *

S: It's called Nisha.

K: Who?

S: The cyclone. It's sitting over Pamban. It's been sitting over Pamban for the last 16 hours.

K: Why would anything sit over Pamban for 16 hours?

S: I thought Pamban was a brand name for cooking oil.

K: If you were having second thoughts about suicide, all you'd have to do is sit in Pamban for 16 hours.

S: It's sitting over Pamban, not in Pamban.

K: You know, sometimes this incense smells like marijuana and sometimes it smells like burnt milk.

S: It's just sitting there and that's why you're flooding.

K: I'm flooding?

* * *

S: The cyclone is now brutalizing parts of Andhra Pradesh. Sun is shining?

K: Sun is shining. Everything smells bad and there's suddenly all these birds.

S: They probably came with the flood. Is the water going down?

K: Yeah, but I hate these birds. There's this supercockyfucker that keeps flying around here. If there's one thing I can't stand it's an arrogant bird.

S: Do you have a gun?

K: Why?

S: You could shoot the supercockyfucker bird.

K: I'm going to go find a rock.

* * *

S: Will you qualify for flood relief? I heard you get money and free rice.

K: If your house washes away you get way more stuff.

S: Well, maybe next time.

K: I think my neighbors are yelling at me about the window.

S: What window?

K: I broke their window when I threw a rock at the supercockyfucker bird. What if my neighbors get violent?

S: Are they a violent people?

K: Well, they are non-vegetarians. And once I saw this cat in their yard and then it wasn't in their yard anymore so I think they probably ate it.

S: I think you should take a rock with you.

K: If I don't call back in an hour, will you call the police?

S: No.

K: OK.

Paruppu Keerai

K: So. What's been happening?

N: Nothing.

K: You know how long you've been sitting here?

N: Just like ten minutes maybe. Four minutes.

K: Two hours.

N: OK.

K: And you still won't eat that paruppu-keerai on your plate.

N: No.

K: Dude, it's like four bites. Just shove it in your mouth and you're done.

N: No.

K: Why are you being so bananas about this?

N: Amma said I drove her up a wall today.

K: That's truly shocking.

N: Why she said like that but.

K: I don't know, let's see. First you decided to cut your own hair.

N: Ya.

K: And then you hid the aforementioned hair in the sofa.

N: Is it nice? My hairstyle?

K: Do you know what nuclear holocaust means?

N: Does that mean it's nice?

K: No dude. It does not.

N: Then I drank ink.

K: Which is just gross.

N: I thought it would be sweet.

K: And now here you are, not allowed to get up from the table until you eat your paruppu-keerai which you refuse to do.

N: What if I go under the table.

K: Go on. See what happens to you.

N: What will happens to me.

K: I will step on you. Repeatedly.

N: I'll tell Amma.

K: After all you've done today, I don't think she'll care.

N: But I don't like paruppu-keerai.

K: I don't like it either but I ate mine and now no one can question me.

N: You eat it then.

K: You eat it.

N: Amma will eat it.

K: Ask her to eat it, right now. Let's see what happens.

N: I eat it tomorrow.

K: Why are you doing this? Just eat it! Just put it in your mouth and it's over!

N: OK.

K: Good.

N: I do it tomorrow.

K: You know what's going to happen? You're going to end up sitting here for the rest of your life. Your butt is going to grow into the chair and your fingers are going to grow into the plate and the paruppu-keerai is going to seep into your skin and have babies.

N: Then what will happen?

K: This is not story-time!

N: Why?

K: OK, I'm going. Say goodbye to your butt.

N: Can I say butt also?

K: No.

N: Can I say bum?

K: OK. Just once though.

* * *

K: Still here I see.

N: Amma sat with me and had tea.

K: Your plate is all dried up and gross.

N: Ya.

K: You do realize that the longer you sit here the worse that's going to taste.

N: When are you going to die?

K: What?

N: What time you're going to die.

K: Why are you asking me that? Do you know something?

N: I'm never going to die.

K: Oh yeah? How are you going to manage that?

N: I'm going to drink lots of water and pray to God all the time and give money to people.

K: Just random people?

N: Ya.

K: Can I have some money then?

N: No. And I will be polite. And sharpen all my pencils.

K: That would be the real key to everlasting life, I'm guessing.

N: Ya.

K: Well, the day is almost at an end. And you've basically just sat here, watching that paruppu-keerai harden into a cold, semi-solid mound of yuck.

N: And I cut my hair.

K: And you drank ink. Let's not forget that one.

N: And I drove Amma up a wall.

K: A satisfying day on the whole I guess.

N: You know what I'm going to do tomorrow?

K: Incite violence among the upper classes? Eat an entire box of crayons?

N: I'm going to make a cake.

K: I don't think you're allowed to use the oven.

N: Out of sand.

K: Oh.

N: And birds.

K: Here we go.

N: And then I put it in the oven.

K: OK, that's it. Just eat the paruppu-keerai or I'm going to stuff it into your ears.

N: I already ate.

K: You di— oh my God, where'd it go?

N: I ate it. Long back ago.

K: Then why are you still sitting here?

N: You didn't have anyone to talk to.

K: Oh my God.

N: I go now but because it's so boring.

K: Did you really eat it or did you put it somewhere weird?

N: Bye.

K: You ate it right? Like a good little person? Little dude?

Marriage

K: Don't ask.

N: Why?

K: Because I don't want to talk about my day, my day was the worst.

N: It was a poo day.

K: That's exactly what it was.

N: Now ask me.

K: Ask you what?

N: About my day.

K: I don't want to know about your day.

N: Ask.

K: I have absolutely no interest in your day little dude.

N: Ask ask.

K: No.

N: I got married.

K: Oh my God.

N: See? I told you ask!

K: Who did you marry?

N: Ezhilarasu.

K: OK. Well at least he has a nice name.

N: Ya.

K: Do I know this Ezhilarasu?

N: He came for my birthday party.

K: Was he the one who kept biting the sofa?

N: No, he was wearing my princess wings.

K: Oh him! Well I'm glad you found a dude who is not afraid to wear princess wings. Does your mom know you're married?

N: No.

K: Aw, you told me first.

N: Ya because you were sitting here.

K: Right. So what's it like being married?

N: It's fine. How come you're not married?

K: Because.

N: Because why.

K: I don't know, I don't feel like it.

N: I don't feel like eating murungaka sambar but Amma says I have to.

K: Ya, it's kind of like that except I don't have to listen to your Amma.

N: My friend Jiah isn't married also.

K: Some people aren't, it's fine. And your friend Jiah is your age so there's that.

N: I'm married but.

K: So you are. Do we get to meet him sometime?

N: Why?

K: I don't know, seemed like the polite thing to say. How come you didn't invite me for the wedding?

N: You were on the phone.

K: So now what are you going to do?

N: I'm going to do drawing.

K: What about your husband?

N: Hm?

K: You don't know where your husband is?

N: No.

K: And this doesn't seem odd to you?

N: Maybe he went home for lunch.

K: Well I wish you both happy married life. Here.

N: What it is.

K: A paperclip.

N: I like Dairy Milk.

K: Well this paperclip is your wedding present. May it bring you much joy and inner peace.

N: OK. You want to give me Dairy Milk?

K: No.

* * *

N: I tell you something.

K: Dude, no.

N: Why?

K: Because you'll say something weird and too many weird things have already happened to me today.

N: But I tell you something.

K: No, don't tell me anything, I don't want to know.

N: I got married.

K: You already told me this and it was bad enough the first time.

N: No, again I got married.

K: Isn't that illegal?

N: I married Jiah.

K: Wow, what happened to Ezhilarasu?

N: Nothing.

K: You guys were like meh, this is boring now.

N: Ya.

K: Why didn't you go for marriage counselling?

N: Actually I forgot.

K: You forgot you were married to Ezhilarasu?

N: Ya but it's fine I think so. Also I lost the paperclip.

K: That's too bad.

N: Anyway it's not a good gift. I like Dairy Milk.

K: So it's you and Jiah now, is it?

N: Ya. She has remote control helicopter.

K: Well that's a good reason to marry someone I guess. What about her personality?

N: Once she sneezed and all this stuff came out of her nose and I saw.

K: Classy.

N: Can I have a Dairy Milk?

K: Why?

N: Because I got married.

K: You do not get a Dairy Milk for getting married.

N: On TV they give.

K: This is not TV land, we've talked about this.

N: But you gave me a paperclip and I didn't like it.

K: Yeah, well life's tough sometimes, always remember that.

N: Chupa Chups?

K: I have no idea what you said just now.

N: Chupa Chups.

K: What does that mean?

N: Can I have a Chupa Chups?

K: No, it sounds problematic.

N: Gems?

K: No.

N: Tic Tac?

K: No.

N: You have to give me something.

K: Go bring Jiah, I'll give you both something.

N: What?

K: It's a surprise.

N: You can't give me paperclip again.

K: Oh. OK, would you like a potato?

N: Can I have a tomato?

K: A tomato? Really?

N: Ya. I like tomatoes. And I like Dairy Milk.

K: OK, then let this tomato be your wedding gift. Wish you happy married life dear.

N: OK but I like Dairy—

K: You're not getting a Dairy Milk dude.

N: I know why. Because life is tough sometimes.

K: That is exactly right.

Be Better

K: Sit down, I have to talk to you.

N: Did you get in trouble?

K: Why would I get in trouble?

N: Maybe because you said bum.

K: When did… I did not say bum. And don't use that as an excuse to say bum when you're not supposed to.

N: You just said bum though.

K: Would you stop saying bum please?

N: You only keep saying bum.

K: Just… OK listen, that's not what I wanted to talk to you about. I need you to listen to me very carefully.

N: When?

K: Right now.

N: Tomorrow.

K: Not tomorrow.

N: I can listen tomorrow.

K: Dude, put your hand over your mouth and don't say anything until I tell you.

N: OK.

K: Now, tomorrow you are going to meet a friend of mine. And maybe you might think that this friend looks a little different.

N: Different than what.

K: Well… like maybe you might think, oh this person looks like a man. And then maybe you might think oh if they look like a man, then they can't wear lipstick.

N: Why not.

K: Well because that's what a lot of people might think, that someone who looks like a man can't wear lipstick.

N: Who people.

K: Like… society.

N: Your friend can wear my lipstick, I don't mind.

K: You don't have any lipstick.

N: You can buy me one.

K: Dude stop derailing the conversation! Now where was I.

N: Your friend wears lipstick.

K: Well, yes. They like to wear lipstick.

N: OK.

K: They also have long hair.

N: OK.

K: I don't think you're getting what I'm saying.

N: Your friend has long hair and a lipstick.

K: Do you… get what that means?

N: Ya.

K: What does it mean exactly?

N: Your friend has long hair and a lipstick.

K: And that means they are…

N: They are your friend.

K: You have to call him 'they'. Them I mean.

N: Because they don't have a name.

K: No no, he has— they have a name.

N: Because their name is so secret.

K: No it's just... dude it's all really confusing for me.

N: Ya.

K: It is, right? I mean I get the whole pronoun thing but—

N: I know what a pronoun is.

K: You do? Really?

N: Ya.

K: I feel like I'm going to call him him instead of them.

N: Like you did just now.

K: Yeah! See? It's so complicated.

N: I lied before though.

K: Hm?

N: I don't know what that p thing is.

K: Listen, maybe it would be better if you didn't meet him actually.

N: Them.

K: Them, right, them.

N: Why?

K: Because you might call him him instead of them.

N: Them.

K: What?

N: You keep saying 'him', it's 'them'.

K: Right, right them.

N: Maybe you shouldn't meet them.

* * *

K: You know what non-binary means?

N: Yes.

K: Wait, what? You do?

N: It's where they keep the books.

K: Dude that's library.

N: Yes.

K: Why am I even talking about this with you?

N: Because you have no friends.

K: What the heck little dude.

N: What is it then?

K: What?

N: The thing you said wasn't a library.

K: Non-binary.

N: Okay. What it is then?

K: I don't know.

N: Why?

K: Because! It's confusing! And I keep forgetting to look it up.

N: You can look it up now.

K: Well… yeah I guess I could.

N: You need help?

K: No, I think I can manage thank you. Okay, so non-binary means when someone isn't male or female.

N: It's not confusing.

K: Well no, not when you say it like that.

N: Now everything is great.

K: Eh?

N: Now you aren't confused and you can see your friend and I can have kaju katli and chips. And lime juice. With ice.

K: I just need to remember to say them. Them them them.

N: It's OK if you make a mistake. They're your friend.

K: That's true.

N: Now everything is great.

K: Well, it's OK I guess.

N: Everything is great.

K: It's mildly satisfactory.

N: Can I have the kajukatlichipslimejuiceice now?

K: No.

N: Can I have a potato?

K: You can have an onion. Deal?

N: Deal.

Aadhi

K: Who did you say was coming?

N: My friend Aadhi.

K: Is he the one you married?

N: No.

K: He bites furniture.

N: No.

K: It's not that weird kid is it? The one who doesn't blink?

N: I can blink. See?

K: That's not blinking, that's… what exactly are you doing with your face?

N: It's blinking.

K: OK, have I met Aadhi before?

N: Ya.

K: Did I like Aadhi?

N: No.

K: Oh my god it's that weird kid.

N: Am I blinking now?

K: Why is he coming here though?

N: To play.

K: But he just stands there. Not blinking. And when he talks I can never understand what he's saying. Sometimes it almost sounds like English and then it almost sounds like Tamil and then it definitely sounds like Russian.

N: I can understand him.

K: I think you just pretend to understand him to make the rest of us look bad.

N: Can I have some mango ice cream?

K: No.

N: What if Aadhi wants me to have?

K: What if Aadhi wants you to have mango ice cream?

N: Ya.

K: Really dude?

N: OK you can give me later.

K: I'm not giving you any mango ice cream. You little extortionist.

N: Hm?

K: Ex-tor-shun-ist.

N: Is that me?

K: Yes.

N: It's nice.

* * *

K: Hi Aadhi, what's happening in your little life? How are your people? I have no idea what you're saying.

N: We are going to play Ghost Ghost. It's going to be so scary bye.

K: OK. Have fun fun. Little dude?

N: Hm?

K: You want to take Aadhi with you?

N: AAAADHIIII!

K: Why don't you come here and get him instead of rupturing everyone's ear drums.

N: AAAADHIIII!!!!

K: Go on Aadhi, don't you want to have fun playing Ghost Ghost Ghost Ghost?

N: AAAADHIIIII!!!

K: No? You just want to stand there? Not blinking?

N: AAAADHIIII!!!

K: What if I offered you money?

N: AADHI COME I'LL DRAW ON YOUR FACE!!!

K: Really? That's a better incentive than money? Maybe it is.

* * *

K: So, you're both ghosts then.

N: Ya, I'm a intervisible ghost.

K: Invisible.

N: OK.

K: And Aadhi is…

N: He's another ghost.

K: Which would explain the sheet which is covering him.

N: We are both so scary.

K: You didn't actually draw on his face, did you? Because I might get in trouble if you did. I mean you might get in trouble.

N: You can't talk to me, I'm a intervisible.

K: OK. And Aadhi, you're just going to stand there? With that sheet over your head? You know, our relationship could be so different if I knew what you were saying.

N: He wants to stand there.

K: Well Aadhi dude, I'm working here so you're going to have to stand somewhere else.

N: You're just looking at your phone.

K: No, I'm doing… stuff.

N: What stuff?

K: I'm… OK fine he can stand there.

N: We're going to dance now.

K: Like right now? OK you mean right now.

N: Is it nice?

K: Aadhi you are as graceful as a gazelle, which is amazing. Little dude, you jump up and down very well.

N: Should we stop now?

K: No, keep going.

N: When are we having the mango ice cream?

K: Never.

N: After lunch.

K: Never does not mean after lunch.

N: Why?

K: Because.

N: I think so it means after lunch.

* * *

K: Where is it all going??

N: He ate it.

K: I just put the rice on his plate. Like a second ago.

N: Aadhi eats fast.

K: Is he inhaling it? It's hard to tell with that sheet over his head.

N: He wants more rice.

K: I don't think there is any more.

N: Why?

K: Because he ate it all. Aadhi you want me to make some more?

N: He says yes.

K: I was kinda hoping he'd say no.

N: We can have mango ice cream also.

K: You really think that's going to happen, don't you.

N: Ya. It's going to happen.

* * *

K: Well Aadhi, it's been a pleasure. You sure you want to keep wearing that bedsheet? I really wish I could understand what you're saying, it sounds so interesting.

N: He said yes.

K: Won't your mom think it's weird if you come home wearing a bedsheet over your head? Guess not.

N: BYE AADHI!!!

K: BYE AADHI!!!

N: Why you yelling?

K: I thought we were all yelling.

N: I'm going to play now.

K: Wait! Tell me about your day with Aadhi, did you have fun?

N: He was sad I didn't get any mango ice cream.

K: Well, life is full of sorrow.

N: Did I draw on his face?

K: What? Why are you asking me that?

N: Hm?

K: You drew on his face didn't you.

N: Ya.

K: Well maybe he won't take that sheet off and it'll be OK.

N: Can you draw on my face?

K: I probably shouldn't.

N: Can you draw a shoe rack?

K: Pretty sure I can't draw a shoe rack. Especially on a face.

N: I bring my markers?

K: Absolutely, let's do this.

Remember When We Were All Friends on Facebook???!!

K: Do you know that Facebook helped me find the girl who sat behind me in college? And I looked at all her photographs. She's posted 57 pictures of her hand but some of them were her kid I think.

S: Her kid looks like a hand?

K: I mean, she found me actually. She remembered my name, and pretty much everything about me.

S: That's... kind of scary.

K: Anyway, I have to go work on my 25 Random Things You Should Know About Me list. I really want it to be funny and irreverent and thought-provoking and serious and heartwarming and edgy and funny.

S: Maybe there's an online tutorial for that. How To Write A 25 Random Things You Should Know About Me List That Is Funny and Irreverent and Thought-Provoking and Serious and Heartwarming and Edgy and Funny.

K: I'm going to go check.

* * *

K: It took me three whole days but it's finally finished.

S: Please please please don't read it to me. Please.

K: Random fact #1. I love running marathons.

S: So you've just straight-up lied on this then.

K: Random Fact #2. I love poor orphans.

S: When have you ever interacted with a poor orphan?

K: Look, if I had to choose between a movie about aliens and a movie about poor orphans, I would choose the orphans. Which is like love.

S: Is it really though?

K: Random Fact #3. I am a medical marvel because I have two hearts and eight livers.

S: Why are you lying like this on a random Facebook list?

K: Because I'm Facebook friends with people who say they've sailed around the world in shoeboxes and built solar-powered cars with chewing gum.

S: Who are these people?

K: I don't really know, they're Facebook friends.

S: So you're making a list of lies to share with people you don't really know.

K: I know the girl who sat behind me in college. Oh my God.

S: What?

K: I sat in the last row in college what the fuck!

S: Oh please don't start talking about back benchers as if they are interesting.

K: I SAT IN THE LAST ROW!

S: I DON'T CARE!

K: THAT MEANS THERE WAS NO ONE SITTING BEHIND ME YOU WALNUT!

S: Oh that's right.

K: Who is this person even?

S: I feel like she's a ghost.

K: How did she know all that stuff about me? *Why* did she know all that stuff about me?

S: The real question is, if she didn't sit behind you, where DID she sit?

K: DON'T SAY THAT

S: You are being haunted by the stalkerghosts of the internet.

K: OK you can just fuck right off.

S: WHERE DID SHE SIT! WHAT ARE YOUR CRIMES! Hello?

I AM
LOVE
FAILURE

Awaiting Vagene and Bobe

SexehBewbies: Someone pinged me on the sex chat thing!

K: As in a human being person someone?

SexehBewbies: Yes!

K: Oh my God.

SexehBewbies: I know! I'm so excited! I GOT PINGED ON THE SEX CHAT!!!!

K: Oh my God.

SexehBewbies: Any idea what happens now?

K: I think you have to chat with them. Like, sexually.

SexehBewbies: I tried.

K: What did you say?

SexehBewbies: I said hi. Then they said hi.

K: And?

SexehBewbies: And that's it. Should I say hi again?

K: Try 'hey sweetie'.

SexehBewbies: Okay, hang on.

K: And?

SexehBewbies: They want me to take my shirt off.

K: Like right now?

SexehBewbies: Yes. Because they are so… hornay?

K: What is that?

SexehBewbies: I don't know, should I ask? Hang on, they're typing something. 'Tell me all the news about your tits'.

K: You should probably tell them you don't have any.

SexehBewbies: I can pretend I have some. FEELING SO HOT WITH ALL MY BOOBIES RIGHT NOW WOW THEY SMELL SO HOT!

K: Wow.

SexehBewbies: I wasn't sure what to say. Now they want to know what they feel like.

K: Say they feel like home.

SexehBewbies: THEY FEEL MOIST AND THEY FEEL LIKE HOME I LOVE MY HOUSE AND MY COUNTRY.

K: And nipples.

SexehBewbies: MY NIPPLES ARE ROLLING ALL OVER MY BOOBS

K: Oh my.

SexehBewbies: They're typing, hang on. 'Touch yourself right now dirty whore.'

K: That's not very nice.

SexehBewbies: I know! YOU ONLY DIRTY WHORE YOU FULL FAMILY DIRTY WHORE SHAME SHAME PUPPY SHAME

K: What are they saying?

SexehBewbies: They're saying that they're going to put their hot coke in my sweet hole.

K: Hot coke sounds gross.

SexehBewbies: I'm not comfortable with this idea of hot coke, to be honest.

K: When I was a kid and I had a cold, my parents would give me warm orange juice. Maybe it's like that.

SexehBewbies: 'Gona motorboat your tatas with my hot coke'.

K: Maybe they have a cold and there's no orange juice.

SexehBewbies: Lemme ask. WHY DO YOU HAVE A HOT COKE DO YOU HAVE A COLD WE CAN CHAT LATER IF YOURE NOT FEELING GOOD

K: Tell them orange juice would probably work better than Coke.

SexehBewbies: Oh, cock! Like penis cock!

K: They want to put their hot penis cock in your sweet hole! OK, that makes sense.

SexehBewbies: They're typing something—'are you touching yourself yet?' MY KNEES ARE TOUCHING IS THAT WHAT YOU MEAN

K: I think they mean sexually bro, not generally.

SexehBewbies: Oh! OK I got this. I AM TOUCHING ALL OF MY BOOB AND NIPPLES THANK YOU FOR ASKING. I want to talk about my vagina now.

K: You don't have one though.

SexehBewbies: MY VAGINA IS SO HARD FOR YOU RIGHT NOW I'M DROPPING

K: I think maybe—

SexehBewbies: I MEAN I'M DROPPING SRY

K: Maybe you should—

SexehBewbies: DROPPING

K: Okay.

SexehBewbies: DROPPING WHY DOES IT KEEP DOING THAT WHAT THE FUCK. Dude why won't it let me write 'dripping'!

K: Maybe because that's not what you're typing.

SexehBewbies: OK they said they're touching themselves but they have to go soon. COOL.

K: What the fuck, don't say cool! Ask them what it's like.

SexehBewbies: You mean like the weather?

K: No, whatever they're touching.

SexehBewbies: Oh! OK: WHAT IS IT LIKE NOT THE WEATHER I MEAN. It's... very long. It is snake. No wait, it's a fish. In the pants.

K: There's a snake fish in his pants?

SexehBewbies: They have sexed so many ladies with their massive... orfan?

K: Aw, orphans are sad.

SexehBewbies: Ah fuck.

K: Oh man! When will the power come back?

SexehBewbies: Oh maybe in... 5 hours.

K: I think we are now in love with whoever that was. Don't you?

SexehBewbies: Yes. I want to have his babies.

K: I want to bend him over a sink and wash his hair. Wish we knew his name.

SexehBewbies: BIGPENIS4U76930285

K: We will sit here and wait for him to come back. And when he does, we will send him pictures of your nude knees. And your bellybutton.

SexehBewbies: AND THEN WE'RE GETTING MARRIED!

The F Word

N: I tell you something so secret?

K: You've just bought 12 kilos of cocaine.

N: Hm?

K: Nothing, you tell me.

N: I know a bad word.

K: Wow.

N: Ya.

K: Where did you learn this bad word?

N: The big kids said it.

K: So what are you going to do with this word?

N: Nothing.

K: Ya? You're just going to keep it in your head?

N: Ya. Because it's a bad word.

K: OK, well that sounds like a good plan.

N: You know any bad word?

K: A few.

N: Say me.

K: Why do you want to learn bad words?

N: Just say me. Please.

K: Um… poosinikai?

N: That's pumpkin.

K: How about tree… leafy.

N: What means tree leafy.

K: It's like when there's like… a tree? And… stuff.

N: What stuff?

K: Just like… leafy stuff.

N: Why is it a bad word?

K: Because tree leafy is like… like if someone said that to me, I'd be like, no, I'm not a tree… leafy.

N: It's like moron.

K: What the heck, where did you learn 'moron' from?

N: From a movie. I tell you the new bad word I learned?

K: I don't know, I—

N: It starts with F.

K: What?

N: Starts with F.

K: The F word? You learned the F word?

N: Ya.

K: Oh my God.

N: Ya.

K: Oh my God.

N: I can say it if you want.

K: Don't don't don't shhh.

N: Because it's so bad.

K: Where did you hear this word?

N: The big kids. And one time you said it.

K: No! You heard me say it?

N: Ya.

K: Dude oh no.

N: You said it on the phone. You said someone was a hecking f—

K: Fish. I said hecking fish.

N: No. You said—

K: Fudge. Formaldehyde. Oh my hecking heck what have I done?

N: You said a bad word.

K: Ya. I'm sorry little dude. You shouldn't know that word.

N: I say it?

K: No. Don't ever say it. Ever.

N: How come you get to say it?

K: Because I'm a big person.

N: You said when I did potty by myself I was a big person.

K: This goes far beyond potty.

N: When I get big I can say bad words?

K: No. Yes. I don't know. I'm going home now, OK? Don't say that word.

N: It's f—

K: Don't! Oh my God!

* * *

N: Hi.

K: Hello.

N: You remember that time when I said to you about some bad word something?

K: No.

N: Some bad word or something I said to you.

K: I know nothing about this. You never said anything to me.

N: Ya I think so I said.

K: This never happened.

N: Why you don't want me to say it.

K: Because there's so many nicer words out there. Like… adhesive.

N: Hm?

K: Adhesive. Say it.

N: Is it a bad word?

K: No, it's a nice, harmless word. Or petrichor. Or borborygmi.

N: What means the fffff bad word.

K: Oh don't do this to me.

N: Does it mean cockroach?

K: Not exactly.

N: Does it mean like hitting someone?

K: It could, I guess. In a way. It's actually a bit complicated.

N: Like so much hitting?

K: No, it's like… I actually have no idea what to say to you right now.

N: Why?

K: Because no one told me what to say when something like this happens.

N: When someone says bad word.

K: When you say bad word.

N: It's OK.

K: Yeah? I feel like I should tell you something useful. Because you're probably going to end up using this word when you're older.

N: Even though it's a bad word?

K: Even though it's a bad word.

N: Why?

K: Because sometimes you might just feel something so much that you just say it.

N: So you have to say bad word?

K: No, you don't have to. Maybe you'll learn some better words to use when you grow up.

N: I say the bad word anyway?

K: Do you absolutely have to?

N: I just say to you, very quiet. I say it in your ear.

N: *whispers*

K: Oh!

N: Ya.

K: You said fool!

N: Shhh!

K: I called someone a hecking fool on the phone?

N: You're keeping on saying it!

K: Oh I'm sorry little dude, you're right it's not the best word. But it's not that bad. I mean you're going to hear words that are a lot worse.

N: Should I tell Amma my bad fffff word?

K: You absolutely should. Right now.

N: OK.

K: Make sure you tell her it's the F word. And you never heard me say it, OK?

N: OK. You said it on the phone but.

K: No I didn't.

N: You did but.

K: Go tell your Amma.

N: You did but.

K: OK, I'm going now.

N: You did.

The Girl

N: I tell you something?

K: Give me money first.

N: You know when I went to that aunty's house because Amma made me go and I didn't want to go because Jiah's kittens and it was raining and I couldn't wear my rain boots because I put sand in them?

K: I should ideally say no but for some reason, I know what you're talking about.

N: Ya in that house you know what I sawed?

K: Wildebeests sweeping majestically across the ceiling.

N: There was a girl.

K: OK. Well that's not very interesting, as you might have guessed.

N: She was in the kitchen.

K: Still not super interesting.

N: She was washing the floor.

K: Oh.

N: Because maybe she spilled something. Right?

K: Well—

N: Or maybe she likes washing.

K: That's probably not why.

N: Why then?

K: I think she works there.

N: Like school.

K: No, not like school. Like, she works. For money.

N: Because there are no big people.

K: I... don't think that's why.

N: Because she likes it.

K: No, little dude, she probably doesn't.

N: Then why?

K: Because... some kids have to work.

N: Why?

K: I guess because their family needs money.

N: What happened to the big people?

K: I don't know, maybe they work too. Or maybe they don't.

N: Is it bad?

K: Kids working like that? Yeah, it's bad.

N: When are we going to tell the police?

K: Um...

N: Because it's bad right? So we have to tell the police. Right?

K: Well it's a little more complicated than that.

N: Why?

K: As in... well, it's complicated because... like, I don't think... I don't know if telling the police is the best idea.

N: Why but.

K: Because... you know, a lot of people have kids working in their houses. A LOT.

N: So we tell the police about all of them.

K: No that's not what we do.

N: What do we do then.

K: Um… nothing, actually.

N: But it's bad you said.

K: It is, it's just… it's like a bad thing that happens even though people know it's bad.

N: What about that girl.

K: She'll be OK. I think. I mean, I'm sure that aunty is nice to her.

N: She makes her wash the floor but.

K: Yeah but that's her job. I mean—

N: But she's a girl.

K: Yeah but… listen, you don't have to worry about all that stuff, OK? It's… hey, where are you going?

N: To my room.

K: You want to talk about this some more?

N: No.

K: You sure? We can… OK, I guess you're sure.

* * *

K: Hey little dude, you're quiet today.

N: Ya.

K: Ya. It's a bad thing I know, kids working like that.

N: And nobody telling the police.

K: That too.

N: But if no one tells the police how will they know it's happening.

K: I think they know. It's just… it's complicated.

N: It's bad.

K: Yeah, and it's bad.

N: We don't do it but.

K: Us? No, we don't do it. At least not anymore.

N: We did before.

K: Well... like when I was growing up, there was this little boy who worked in the house. And there was this girl who helped look after the kids. A lot of people did it, little dude. I mean, it was wrong but... I don't know, it just happened.

N: Why you did like that?

K: I didn't do it, the adults back then did it. But yeah, it was bad, they shouldn't have done that.

N: And no one told the police.

K: That's true, no one did.

N: And now no one is telling the police.

K: That's true but listen, there are organisations and NGOs and things now which help kids like that, they'll make sure they are taken care of.

N: So we don't have to do anything.

K: No, I mean, like we know it's wrong and we don't do it anymore and that's good! And besides that there are organisations to take care of this kind of... stuff.

N: But it's happening but.

K: Yeah, but I mean there are organisations... and they'll take care of everything. Oh! And we can give money to the organisations, to help them help those kids.

N: Do we give money?

K: Sure! I mean, like I donated a while back, I think. Or was that for the floods? Anyway, doesn't matter, the point is we can give money to help. As in we can give money to other people so they will help.

N: And we don't have to do anything.

K: Well, giving money is something. No?

N: I get my money now?

K: You have money?

N: Thaathaa gave me, I get now?

K: Oh no, you don't have to give your money, you keep that. Save it for something nice.

N: But what about helping?

K: That... you don't worry about that, the big people will do all that, OK?

N: Really you will?

K: Sure! And listen, I'll talk to Amma, you don't have to go to that aunty's house anymore OK?

N: Why?

K: Because seeing that girl makes you upset.

N: Because it's bad.

K: Yeah, but you don't have to worry about that anymore. And I'll donate some money to CRY or something right now. OK? Sound good?

N: I'm going down.

K: You're off to play then?

N: I just want to go.

K: OK. But don't worry about all this stuff anymore, OK? It's all good. I'll donate some money and it'll all be fine. OK?

N: Bye.

K: It'll be fine, little dude. Trust me. Everything's fine.

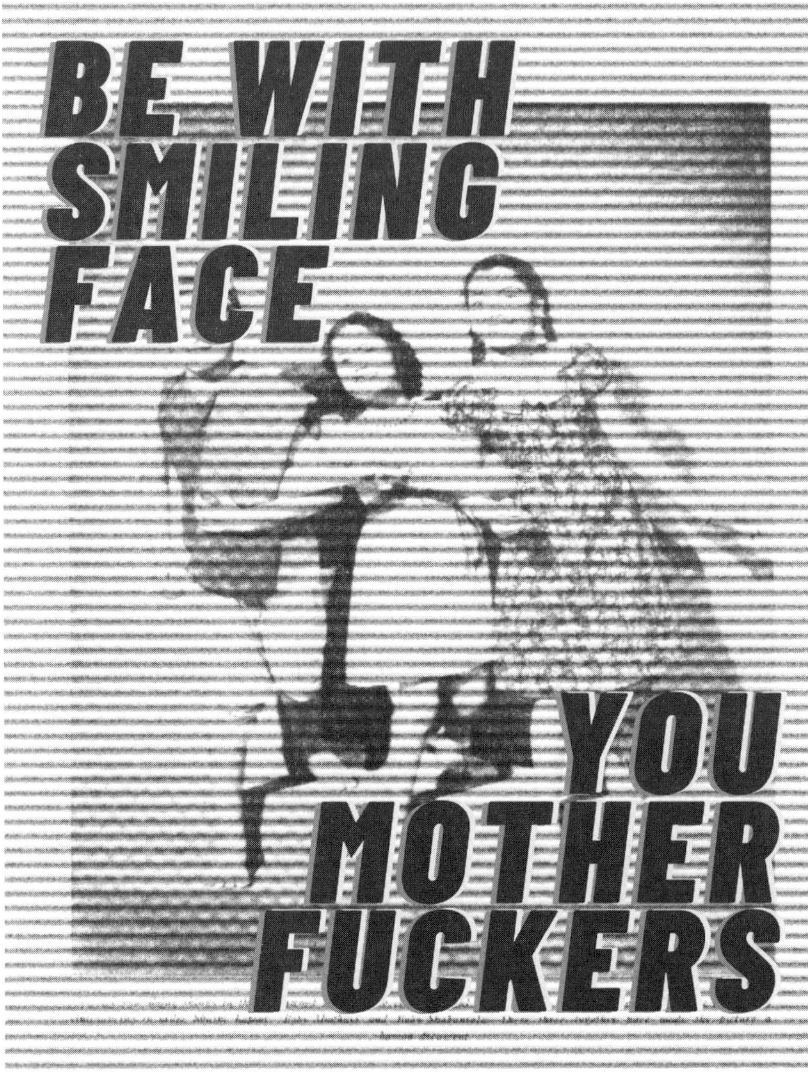
BE WITH
SMILING
FACE
YOU
MOTHER
FUCKERS

Don't Even Talk to Me Right Now Oh My God

K: I just can't. It was So. Disturbing. I can't even tell you how disturbing it was. I am so disturbed by how disturbing it was.

S: Well I have to go anyway so—

K: Ask me what was so disturbing.

S: Actually I have to—

K: So as you may know, I'm a bit of a connoisseur of Japanese cinema.

S: I don't think watching one video by Dir En Grey makes you a connoisseur of Japanese cinema.

K: Bro, I'm into so many facets of Japenese culture. For instance, I'm super into ani… mals?

S: Try that again. I dare you.

K: Ani... mation.

S: Anime! Anime Anime Anime!

K: That's animation only.

S: Oh my God.

K: Anyway, I finally watched 'Imprint'! It's a Japanese horror movie type thing that they wouldn't show on American TV because it was so disturbing!

S: Yeah so I don't want to hear about that.

K: Yeah, it was pretty disturbing. I don't think you could handle that much disturbingness.

S: Cool. Anyway, have to go now so—

K: Call me later though and I'll tell you what was so disturbing.

* * *

K: You never called so I thought I should call you myself to tell you what was so disturbing in the Japanese horror movie type thing. There was this scene where they tortured this geisha—

S: Dude I don't want to know.

K: Don't tell lies. You DO want to know but you're putting scene.

S: I'm not putting scene, I really don't want to know. Let's talk about non-Japanese horror movie type things.

K: Can we talk about geishas?

S: No.

K: Can we talk about Japanese culture?

S: What do you know about Japanese culture?

K: I know they have geishas. Let's talk about geishas.

S: If you even say the word 'geishas', I'm hanging up.

K: But geishas are a part of Japanese culture, it's racist not to talk about them. Hello? Did you just hang up on me? Bro.

* * *

K: Hi. I don't want to talk about geishas.

S: Glad to hear it.

K: Can we talk about sewing?

S: What in God's name would you have to say about sewing?

K: I want to talk about needlepoint. I want to talk about how there are needles in needlepoint.

S: So?

K: There are also needles in the torture scene in the Japanese horror movie type thing and they stick them into this woman's—

S: No.

K: But I didn't even say 'geishas'!

S: You can't talk about needles anymore.

K: Can I talk about incense?

S: No.

K: Fine. Then I won't tell you about how in the torture scene in the Japanese horror movie type thing they burned this woman with incense and— Hello? Did you hang up on me again? Bro.

* * *

K: You hung up on me again.

S: What part of 'No' do you not understand?

K: I thought maybe you meant 'Yes' when you said 'No'.

S: You're not allowed to talk to me about geishas, needles or incense.

K: Then you talk about something.

S: OK, let's talk about who I saw today. Remember that girl from college who used to eat six samosas every day?

K: The one with the twin?

S: No no, remember she would never share because she said she would faint if she didn't eat six samosas a day?

K: She had a twin, no?

S: What the fuck, stop saying she had a twin! She ate all those samosas man!

K: Funny you should mention twins.

S: I didn't mention twins, what's wrong with you?

K: There was a parasitic twin in the Japanese horror movie type thing which was actually this little face in the middle of a hand which lived on this geisha's head don't hang up on me. Hello?

S: Yes?

K: You didn't hang up on me!

S: That's because I wanted to tell you that you're not allowed to talk to me about anything ever again.

K: Can I talk about this little girl with blue hair who had a parasitic twin living on her head if I don't mention that the little girl grows up to be a geisha? Hello? Bro.

Hindi Is the Mother Tongue of India

S: No you fucking don't.

K: Yes I do.

S: Bro, you know those foreigners who think people in India speak Hindu?

K: Yeah.

S: Those people know more Hindi than you do.

K: Not all those people.

S: Most of them.

K: OK most of them.

S: Also just need to mention that HINDI IS NATIONAL LANGUAGE!!!

K: HINDI IS MOTHER TONGUE OF ALL REAL MOTHERS!!!!!

S: HINDI HAS A PERSISTENT RASH ON ITS B—

K: No.

S: THAT is crossing the line??

K: You can't talk about persistent rashes bro, come on.

S: Well you can fuck off with all that anyway because Thamizhan da.

K: Aamanga.

S: THAMIZHAN DA!!

K: AAAMAAANGA!!

S: HINDI MANAANGAATI NONSENSE!!

K: I do feel like I know Hindi though.

S: Do you though?

K: Intuitively I know Hindi.

S: Do you remember that time you insisted that 'diwani' was the feminine form of 'divan'?

K: That's because it is.

S: Dude.

K: How can that be wrong?? Y'all just lying about that one.

S: There was also that time you kept saying that 'mehboob' meant 'my boob'.

K: How can 'mehboob' NOT mean 'my boob', that's just bananas. BANANAS I TELL YOU.

S: And you were actually telling people this LIKE YOU KNEW WHAT YOU WERE TALKING ABOUT.

K: Or—

S: No.

K: Or—

S: FUCK OFF

K: Maybe it means a boob that isn't very exciting. Meh boob.

S: Dude there are so many more embarrassing examples of how you absolutely do not know Hindi. Like, at all.

K: That is your opinion bro.

S: For instance, 'Jo nahin kaha hai' does not mean 'Joe is not here, where is Joe.'

K: It should though, right?

S: 'Meri jaan' does not mean 'my toilet'.

K: Well why not then.

S: And my personal favourite, that golden time in your very dangerous youth, when you had the ever-loving audacity to tell the Light Music Team in college that you knew the Hindi lyrics to 'Chinna Chinna Asai'.

K: Because I did.

S: You actually stood there and said hey ya'll I know the lyrics, let me show you.

K: Yes.

S: Then you opened your mouth and said—

K: I said the right thing.

S: 'Buskee Boori Osha, Biskee Baree Asha'.

K: Yes.

S: The line is 'Dil hai chhota sa, chhoti si asha, masti bhare mann ki, bholi si asha'.

K: That only I said.

S: You said something about biscuits and busking with Asha.

K: Hey you know what happened to me once though? I asked this person, who I thought was my friend, what 'khush naseebi' meant. It's from that song 'Pal' by KK you know.

S: I really don't want to hear this.

K: And he goes 'You know what "pal" means?' And I said yes because I felt like I would probably figure that out later, you know?

S: IYO DA GOD

K: Then he goes 'You know what "kal" means?' And I was like okay sure because I felt like I almost knew what it meant?

S: Fuck. My. Hair.

K: Then he goes 'OK. See first there is "pal". Then there is "kal". So when there is "pal" and "kal", that only is "khush naseebi".'

S: Wow.

K: I don't talk to him anymore. I mean I do but in principle I don't.

S: I don't know what to say.

K: Wouldn't it be neat if 'badi' meant 'buddy'? Like 'friendo' buddy I mean. 'Badi badi aankhen' would be 'friendo friendo eyes'.

S: SAAMI!

K: I also like to think that 'yeh dil jo pyar karega' means 'this is the dill pickle Jo was having sex with when the car came'. And 'salaam-e-ishq' means 'I love processed meats, particularly salami'. Hello? Bro? Ah fuck you anyways.

Fucking Hipsters I Hate How You Make Me Feel!!!

K: You're talking about the underwear, right?

S: What?

K: Hipster. You're talking about the underwear, yes?

S: No.

K: Okay.

S: I'm scared to ask what you thought that whole 'hipster racism' conversation was about.

K: I thought white supremacist lingerie or something.

S: Anyway the hipsters I was talking about are a kind of American. Or they're mostly American. Or something. I'm not really sure what they are.

K: You talk about Americans way too much. I bet Americans don't talk about you half as much as you talk about them.

S: Did you know they say racist things but they say those things because they're NOT racist? It's an actual thing! What would be the difference between hipsters and actual racists though?

K: Who cares? We live in India! Who cares about Americans and their white supremacist lingerie?

S: But what if one of them came here?

K: They'll get loose motion and go home.

S: Oh my God.

K: What?

S: I just remembered this show I saw where they described a dance as having very loose motion.

K: Oh my God.

S: I know! I couldn't watch the rest because 'loose motion' seemed to be a very popular way of describing this particular form of dance. Anyway, I'm going to go figure out this hipster racism thing.

K: Please do. White supremacist lingerie Americans is such a serious problem in India right now.

* * *

S: Look, what would you do if an American hipster came here and said something racist to you and you retaliated because you didn't know that person was actually not racist? I mean how embarrassing would that be!

K: I'd actually shake them down for money.

S: What?

K: Seriously, I do that to all the foreigners I meet.

S: Even the NRIs?

K: Especially the NRIs.

S: What the fuck bro?

K: One time I told this guy that I had sold my kidney and needed money to buy it back. I even showed him a scar.

S: That's… actually pretty great.

K: Yeah, the scar was on my arm but it all worked out in the end.

S: Is being mean to foreigners and NRIs racist?

K: No.

S: I feel like it is though.

K: It probably is.

S: How come I don't feel bad?

K: Because it isn't racist actually.

S: By the way, I tried to find out about hipster racism and went down a hipster panties rabbit-hole. I know way too much about moisture wicking right now.

K: Bro you've made me really anxious about the possibility of encountering hipster racism and thinking it's actual racism. HOW ARE WE SUPPOSED TO DEAL WITH SITUATIONS LIKE THIS

S: Come, let me tell you about moisture wicking in hipster underwear.

K: Will it make me feel better?

S: No.

KINDLY
REFRAIN
FROM
EATING
THE
BABIES

Tragedy of Poverty in Our Society!!!

K: I'm just saying you should have asked me before buying that laptop.

S: Because you could have got me an even better one.

K: Yes.

S: For 23 paisa.

K: Yes.

S: Why do I even talk to you?

K: I seriously can. Company piece, full anti-virus with twelve English movie DVDs that haven't been released abroad yet. With free bag.

S: No warranty? I'm disappointed.

K: If you want a 10-year complete warranty on everything you have to pay two paisa extra.

S: Are you familiar with the term 'liar liar pants on fire'.

K: I just know the right dealers, bro. And these dealers have godowns.

S: I also know dealers who have godowns and none of them sell laptops for 23 paisa.

K: It's my skills that kills.

S: Did those words really just come out of your mouth right now?

K: Listen, I do have a technique, if that's what you want to know.

S: I do want to know. I want to know how you bring a laptop price down from several thousands of rupees to 23 paisa.

K: Well I'm not telling because you're acting too smart.

S: I know, you do that thing where your mouth hangs open and it looks like you're going to sneeze and it makes everyone super uncomfortable so they do whatever you say. What the fuck, did you just fart?

K: It's my laugh.

S: Is that what that is.

K: I laugh like this and I can make an auto driver take me round and round the city twice with one unnecessary drop at Guduvancheri. Guess how much I will pay. Guess guess.

S: No.

K: Two rupees.

S: I can go round and round the city four times with two unnecessary trips to Neelankarai and one unnecessary drop at Guduvancheri for one rupee.

K: I bought an iPhone for 50 paisa and I get everything on it for free all the time forever.

S: I found an iPhone on the road that has everything on it for free all the time forever.

K: My dental work picks up WiFi signals so every time I touch something, it becomes internet-enabled. Like if I touch a toaster. Or a plastic spoon. Or a fish.

S: Imagine if I had actually taken you laptop shopping. Imagine what would have happened.

K: If I'm honest, I feel like I would have encouraged you to make bad choices.

S: Yes.

K: But you would have gotten a good deal on the laptop.

S: And internet-enabled fish. Internet. Enabled. Fish.

K: Oh fuck off.

Good and Bad

K: Oh nice, you've done another drawing! Walk us through it if you will, what is going on in this… whatever this is.

N: It's a fight. This is the good person, this is the shoe rack and this is the bad person.

K: Why is there a shoe ra… never mind. Why does this look like a purple balloon?

N: It's a bad person.

K: Why are they purple though?

N: Bad people are purple.

K: They are?

N: Ya. See in my comic book?

K: He does look a little purple, doesn't he.

N: Why like that?

K: Why like what?

N: Why are bad people always purple?

K: Bad people aren't always purple.

N: They are in this book.

K: Well this book is—

N: And this one.

K: Well—

N: And all these ones. And that one.

K: Well I—

N: Sometimes they are brown though. Like you.

K: OK so I'm brown. But do you think that means I'm a bad person?

N: Sometimes you tell me wrong things Amma said.

K: Apart from that.

N: Why are they brown and purple in books then.

K: I don't know. Seems like bad people can be all sorts of different colours, no?

N: Maybe they didn't have enough colour pencils.

K: What colour are all the good people in these books?

N: Pink.

K: Well, do you think you're good?

N: Ya.

K: Are you pink?

N: Ya.

K: Dude, you're not pink.

N: Ya I am.

K: Who told you you're pink?

N: I did. What should I draw next?

K: I would like to see another… what is this again?

N: Fight. And shoe rack.

K: Right, I would like to see another one like this except without purple bad people and pink good people. Because skin colour doesn't determine if you're good or bad, right?

N: Hm?

K: Just because someone is purple doesn't mean they are bad. Right?

N: Ya.

K: Right.

N: Only if they are brown.

K: No, not if they are brown or purple. I mean pink people can be bad people too.

N: Hm?

K: Am I confusing you?

N: Ya.

K: Forget it, just draw another one.

N: What means confusing?

K: This. All this. This entire conversation with you is confusing.

* * *

K: Hey, what happened to my drawing.

N: I can't finish it.

K: Aw, don't say that. Come on, show me what you've done so far.

N: See.

K: OK. This is the… the…

N: Shoe rack.

K: Of course. But where's the good guy and the bad guy?

N: They went home.

K: No they didn't, come on. Draw a pink bad guy and a purple good guy! Wouldn't that be neat?

N: I don't want to draw, you tell me a story about clouds.

K: Meh, do I have to?

N: Ya.

K: OK once upon a time there was a little cloud and the cloud went wandering outside when her Amma told her not to and she came across this big, black cloud with lightning teeth and—

N: Was he a bad cloud?

K: Probably but anyway, he—

N: Is that why he's black?

K: He… oh heck. OK wait a minute.

N: Is he going to eat the little cloud?

K: No! Because… he was… actually her friend! And he… he had a toothache.

N: And he lost his shoe rack.

K: Right, he had a toothache and he lost his shoe rack so the little cloud helped him and he felt better and they lived happily ever after.

N: So small story?

K: Yes.

N: I didn't like it.

K: Ya but it taught you that just because a cloud is black doesn't mean he's the bad guy.

N: Hm?

K: What does a black cloud mean?

N: Means it's raining.

K: OK that's it, I'm done.

N: Did he find his shoe rack?

K: Yes.

N: Was it in his house?

K: Yes.

N: Then how come he couldn't find it before?

K: You know what little dude? You're giving me a headache.

N: I'm going to draw the cloud and his shoe rack.

K: Don't make him black though.

N: You said he was black.

K: I mean… never mind.

N: I don't have black.

K: Great! Then you can colour him—

N: I draw two shoe racks then.

K: Whatever.

I Am A Boss Babe and These Are My Boss Babe Pants!!!

S: So what exactly does your spiritual movement do?

K: It will turn you into a whole new person.

S: Who?

K: What do you mean, who?

S: Who will it turn me into?

K: Nobody, you'll still be you. But you'll be a better you.

S: That's super disappointing.

K: It's the Developmentalization of the Inner YouYou.

S: Why are there yo-yos in your spiritual movement?

K: YouYou!

S: I don't know what that is.

K: It is That and only That which is not everything and not nothing. But it is something.

S: Can I have a yo-yo? I've never had a yo-yo before.

K: It is an investment in the future of tomorrow today for tomorrows of the future.

S: Today.

K: Yes.

S: Hey you know those ads that say 'for curing gas firstnight marriage piles so many treatment NRIgovernmentofficer successful'.

K: Yes.

S: You think they work?

K: Why are you asking me this?

S: What?

K: What?

S: You only what.

K: What is happening right now?

S: OK I'm going now bai.

* * *

K: So I had the feeling that you weren't completely on board with my spiritual movement idea because you hadn't heard any testimonials.

S: THAT'S why you thought I wasn't on board?

K: Anyway, I thought I'd share one with you— Testimonial #1. 'Everything she said was true and now I am awesome. Other people think I am awesome also.'

S: Who is this person?

K: Lakshmi.

S: Who Lakshmi?

K: B. Lakshmi.

S: I think you made that testimonial up.

K: Why?

S: Because it's stupid.

K: Ok wait, I have another one. Testimonial #2. 'I DevelopMentalized my Inner YouYou and I have dissolved my ego and learned to love myself. I have also discovered that I can talk to certain root vegetables.'

S: Which root vegetables?

K: That's a really intrusive question. Watermelons.

S: You think watermelons are a root vegetable.

K: They have roots.

S: Ok you need to fuck off right now.

K: WATERMELONS HAVE ROOTS I'M NOT LYING— hello? Bro.

* * *

K: OK, forget the testimonials.

S: HOW CAN I EVER FORGET THE TESTIMONIALS

K: I will now easily demonstrate why you need to join my spiritual movement. Let's talk about your life goals.

S: Ew fuck off.

K: My awesome spirituality talents tell me that you have not achieved your life goals.

S: I don't have any life goals.

K: What?

S: I don't have any life goals. I'm allergic.

K: OK, well what about things that you really really want?

S: You want me to tell you what I want? What I reallyreally want?

K: Yes.

S: I'll tell you what I want what I reallyreally want, I wanna HUH I wanna HUH

K: I kind of just walked into that though.

S: I want an elephant actually. I have a friend who grew up in her ancestral home and they had a temple and an elephant and this elephant would come down the road and meet the girl's school bus after school and they would walk back home together GAH! I want that life.

K: You just made that up.

S: No. Can you give me an elephant.

K: Maybe not right now—

S: COWARD!

K: Ooooh wait! I can make you have money. And then you can use that to get your elephant.

S: Does 'make you have money' mean you're going to give me money?

K: No.

S: Feels like it should.

K: Now the first step in attaining your elephant would be to manifest your elephant reality in tandem with the elephant vibrations of the elephant universe.

S: What in the actual fuck.

K: If you don't know how to do that, then you give me money and I will tell you. Guaranteed results.

S: You can guarantee I'll get an elephant?

K: No, I can guarantee there will be results. I have no idea what those results will be though obviously because lol I'm not Spiderman.

S: Spiderman can't predict the future.

K: Oh my God no one cares!

S: Ok so your spiritual movement sucks. And I still don't have an elephant or a yo-yo.

K: Would you like to hear a collection of religious hymns from my spiritual movement?

S: NO!

K: I had no idea you could rhyme so many things with Youyou. Tutu, for example. Shoeshoe. Hello? Bro.

I LIKE NETHILI FISH
I LOVE GEORGE BUSH

I Love You But I Hate You!!!

S: It's ridiculous! We never talk about anything serious or relevant, it's just nonsense from start to finish. If anyone overheard these conversations, they'd say we were—

K: Amazing.

S: No.

K: Very amazing.

S: No.

K: They'd say oh wow you guys are very amazing.

S: See? That's exactly what I'm talking about. Stop saying things like that!

K: I will not deny my amazingness just because it makes you uncomfortable.

S: I am not going to have a conversation with you about any more of that weird shit that comes out of your brain. No more squirrel AIDS or—

K: Squirrel AIDS is serious man, I saw it on YouTube.

S: For once, I would like to talk about something with intellectual maturity and depth.

K: You mean like science? But I don't know science.

S: Do you have anything serious, relevant or important to say? About anything?

K: Never!

S: Well call me when you do.

* * *

S: So obviously the 'serious relevant important' conversations aren't happening.

K: Well I tried to think about science but then I started thinking about—

S: NO!

K: Ok nemmind.

S: How about we talk about normal things in a normal way? Maybe if we stick to normal things the conversations will stay normal.

K: We can certainly try that.

S: Tell me what you did today.

K: Oh! I… nothing.

S: Say pa.

K: I don't think I should.

S: Tell me and I'll decide whether we should pursue the conversation further.

K: I was trying to make candy by melting some old Bournvita.

S: Ugh I've told you not to do that because it's gross.

K: And at some point my neighbour auntie's nightie—

S: Nope. Stop.

K: And then her hair caught fire.

S: Call me if something normal happens.

* * *

S: Do you have normal conversations with other people?

K: Sure. They talk about stuff and when I get bored I hang up.

S: Ah. So this is why you have no friends.

K: That's your opinion. In my opinion I have very much friends.

S: Do you have any friends though.

K: No.

S: OK, let's talk about the budget.

K: Why?

S: Because it's normal, serious, important and relevant to our daily lives. What do you think about the budget?

K: I think it's neat how the words 'bud' and 'get' come together to form the word 'budget', especially when there is no 'j' sound in either 'bud' or 'get'.

S: What books have you read lately?

K: I don't like reading, it hurts my ankles.

S: So I am not going to encourage that line of conversation and instead I'm going to tell you about a book I've read. I'm going to tell you about this book and we're going to have a normal, intelligent conversation about it. OK?

K: OK.

S: This book was about a guy—

K: What was his name?

S: I can't remember.

K: Was it Hepzibah?

S: No.

K: Isn't that neat how you can't remember what the name was but you can remember what it wasn't? Imagine if that was how we introduced ourselves. Hi, My Name Isn't Hepzibah.

S: You're doing it again.

K: Isn't it neat how your name isn't Hepzibah and my name isn't Hepzibah? We have that in common. Same pinch. In school, some girls used to say same pinch kreech-kreech. What is a kreech-kreech?

S: Bro?

K: Ya?

S: Fuck you.

K: OK.

S: Fuck you so, so hard.

Fuck Yeah I'm a Complan Boy!!!

K: Guess how many. Just guess.

S: No.

K: Six. I drank six different kinds of health drinks in my youth!

S: And STILL you didn't get the first rank!

K: It must have done something. All that liquid health just going in and not doing what it was supposed to do?

S: Do you have a tail?

K: What the fuck?

S: Do you have two tails?

K: Listen, all these health drinks were supposed to turn me into an awesome athlete, an awesome cricketer, an awesome scientist and an awesome Bharatanatyam dancer. And all they did was give me gas mostly.

S: I absolutely did not need to know that.

K: My athletics career began and ended with March Past.

S: I got kicked out of March Past because I thought it was 'March Fast' so I was like, isn't that like running? Apparently it wasn't.

K: Ok, so we both lost out in the Athletics Division. Why did you not excel at cricket.

S: Because cricket is for boys.

K: So that's not really the health drink's fault, that's our fault for being ladies.

S: FUCKING LADIES

K: I can't figure out why I didn't become an amazing scientist though! I mean health drinks aside, I was awesome at science!

S: Bro.

K: I had the potential to be awesome at science.

S: Bro!

K: I used to like plants?

S: That doesn't mean you're awesome at science.

K: Fucking hate plants now though.

S: I didn't take science group in school.

K: Aw, what was wrong with you?

S: What.

K: Something was wrong with you, no? Otherwise why you wouldn't take science group?

S: Moving on, that leaves the Bharatanatyam Division, which is something all Real Indian Women should excel at, no?

K: So I was a Bharatanatyam dancer in the sense that I used to sit beside a girl who used to do Bharatanatyam. She kept accusing me of staring at her which was creepy because most of the time, I didn't even know she was there.

S: Feel like we can't really call that Bharatanatyam. Or any form of dance really.

K: I do wonder where all those years of health drink healthiness went.

S: It's probably all accumulated in our elbows or something.

K: What if they did work though? Like, what if this was the best that they could do with us?

S: I CAN DO NO MORE, sobbed the Complan in tones of utter defeat, its tin shuddering under the weight of its failure.

K: I feel bad for the Complan now.

S: I CAN DO NO MORE!!

Best Friends

N: It's Masterchef Masterchef.

K: You mean all this is Masterchef Masterchef? These leaves, this rock and… is that a dead butterfly?

N: It's also Beauty Parlour Beauty Parlour.

K: So this is Masterchef Masterchef Beauty Parlour Beauty Parlour.

N: Ya.

K: Are there two Masterchefs? And two Beauty Parlours?

N: Hm?

K: Why is everything named twice?

N: You can have Manchurian and Butterscotch.

K: I'm afraid to ask.

N: Pizzas.

K: Oh gosh.

N: Also injections.

K: I see you actually have a large purple needle here. Filled with… little bits of confetti I think. And little blue hearts, aw.

N: I give it in your neck.

K: Don't you da— Ow!

N: It's 12 rupees.

K: You want me to pay you for doing that?

N: It's 20 rupees.

K: That's not how that works.

N: I give you another injection.

K: No!

N: Why?

K: Because… I can't think of a good reason actually.

N: I bake you a cake.

K: That's a much better idea. What's with the butterfly?

N: He's sleeping.

K: Are you sure? Seems like he's… not sleeping. Like, dead not sleeping.

N: He's my best friend.

K: That is both weird and sad. Don't you have a human best friend?

N: No.

K: You should probably get a human friend.

N: Why?

K: It's something people say, like you should eat vegetables.

N: I made you a sandwich.

K: What happened to my cake?

N: It's a sandwich.

K: So you're saying this isn't a rock with two leaves on it.

N: No.

K: Great, I'll eat this later.

* * *

N: See this.

K: Hey, it's your allegedly sleeping friend.

N: Ya.

K: I see he's still sleeping.

N: He was awake just now.

K: Are you really sure about that?

N: Ya he just flew around. And ate rice. He's going to bed now.

K: OK. And when you say that you don't mean in your bed, right?

N: Don't make loud noise.

K: You're not keeping that in your bed are you? Little dude?

* * *

N: Did you see my best friend?

K: Recently? No, why?

N: I don't know.

K: Isn't he sleeping? Allegedly?

N: I think he went for a walk.

K: Yeah, I don't think so.

N: I think he went for a walk in the fridge.

K: Did you put that butterfly in the fridge?

N: Hm?

K: You put that butterfly in the fridge didn't you.

N: Yes.

K: Dude that's gross!

N: It was hot.

K: You better take it out before your mom finds it.

N: Ya.

K: What do you mean ya.

N: I can't find him.

K: You've lost your allegedly sleeping butterfly in the fridge.

N: Someone ate him.

K: If I look in that fridge and find it in the curd or something I'll—

N: Did you ate him?

K: Actually I think I'll just go home now.

* * *

K: I see your friend has returned from his sojourn in the fridge.

N: He's still sleeping. Is he sick?

K: Like I said before, he seems to be more dead than anything else.

N: Should I put Vicks on him?

K: You've already done this haven't you.

N: Yes.

K: Well, at least he won't be congested.

N: When will he wake up?

K: I don't think he's going to wake up.

N: In ten minutes?

K: Probably not.

N: He'll be like this all the time?

K: Only until he starts to disintegra— never mind.

N: Can I also be dead?

K: No.

N: Am I dead now?

K: Closing your eyes doesn't make you dead.

N: If I lie down?

K: Why don't you hang out with your other friends now. Like, the human ones. Who aren't so dead all the time.

N: But he's my best friend.

K: He doesn't have to be, you know. Consider the benefits of a human friend. That's alive and all.

N: But I can keep him in my pocket. And I can give him injection.

K: You can do that with human friends.

N: I can?

K: Yes. No. Probably no. I never told you that OK? Someone else did.

N: Can I give you injection?

K: No.

N: Can I give you two injection?

K: Yeah, go on then.

* * *

K: So how's your best friend doing? Haven't seen him lately.

N: He's fine.

K: Still allegedly sleeping?

N: He's swimming.

K: You didn't put him in the water jug, did you?

N: He's in his swimming pool. See?

K: This is a rock in a plastic mug.

N: He's my best friend.

K: It looks suspiciously like the same rock you once said was my sandwich.

N: His name is Coloured Pencil.

K: What happened to the allegedly sleeping butterfly?

N: You ate him.

K: I did not!

N: I ate him.

K: Hahaha what? You didn't actually eat him, did you?

N: Hm?

K: Did you eat that butterfly?

N: I have to put Coloured Pencil in the fridge now.

K: You didn't eat your butterfly best friend, did you? You didn't, right? Dude?

The Dress

N: There.

K: Yup. There it is. Wow.

N: It's my princess dress.

K: I know, it just looks a little… different. On Aadhi.

N: Ya. Because he's Aadhi.

K: Right. And Aadhi dude you're wearing that to the birthday party, are you?

N: He says yes.

K: Did he though? It sounded like something gurgling.

N: Should he wear wings but?

K: Um… you know, about this dress thing—

N: I think he should wear wings.

K: Well why don't we ask Aadhi what he wants. Aadhi, do you really, really, REALLY, want to wear that dress to the birthday party?

N: And wings. He says yes.

K: It sounds different than the noise he made before. Aadhi dude, nod like this if you really want to wear the dress.

N: And wings.

K: Are you sure? Like really sure?

N: See? He wants to.

K: Why do I feel like I'm going to get in trouble for this?

N: Why? Did you say bum?

K: Some people might not like him wearing a dress.

N: Why?

K: Because… well, some people might be like oh he's a boy why is he wearing your dress?

N: Because he doesn't have a dress.

K: Aadhi, you realize some people might say mean things to you? Or make fun of you? For wearing a dress?

N: Who people?

K: Like, I feel so many people. So so many people.

N: I thought you said boys could wear dresses. Your friend wears dresses you said.

K: Yeah but… I mean this is different.

N: Because Aadhi doesn't have a beard.

K: No because… Aadhi, listen. Let me call your mom and ask her.

N: Ask her what?

K: If he can wear your princess dress to the party.

N: Is it bad?

K: No, it's just… let me ask her. I think your mom's number is—

N: Aadhi's mom is in Thailand.

K: Oh. It might be weird if I called her in Thailand to ask if it was OK if her son wore your princess dress to a birthday party. No?

N: You said it wasn't bad.

K: It's not dude, really. It's just… whose party is it?

N: Aaryan.

K: OK let me call his mom and ask if it's OK.

N: I'm also wearing a dress but.

K: Yeah, that's not what people will have a problem with though.

N: You said it wasn't bad.

K: Dude, it is not bad. No matter what happens with this, Aadhi wearing a dress is not bad, OK? Now which one is Aaryan's mom, do I like her?

N: No.

K: Great. This should be a fun conversation.

* * *

K: Oh my hecking god.

N: What she said.

K: That was the longest hecking phone call of my entire life.

N: What she said but.

K: Well, after having a family conference which, for some reason, involved assorted second cousins in Delhi, it was decided that Aadhi shouldn't be allowed to wear a dress to the party.

N: Why but.

K: Because it might make other boys wear dresses too? It's unclear bro.

N: We bring dresses for everyone then.

K: What do they think this is, some kind of viral fever?

N: Are they mad I'm wearing a dress too?

K: No, you're fine. And they seem fine with Aadhi wearing wings. As long as he's wearing pants or shorts with it.

N: But I can't wear pants or shorts.

K: No, you can.

N: Why.

K: I don't know. There are those who think you can't wear pants or shorts though. FYI.

N: We should wear nothing.

K: No, definitely not that. Ever.

N: I don't know what's happening.

K: So here's the deal. Aadhi can wear the wings, pants or shorts but no dress. You can wear anything.

N: I wear my plastic bag dress then.

K: You can't wear that.

N: You said—

K: Dude that's literally just a plastic bag, you cannot wear a plastic bag to a party. Your mom will shave off my eyebrows.

N: Can I shave off my eyebrows?

K: No.

N: Can I shave off Aadhi's eyebrows?

K: No dude what the heck?

N: Aadhi wants to wear the dress but.

K: Aadhi, you can totally wear the dress anytime here, whenever you want.

N: OK.

K: But if you want to go to the party—

N: We stay here.

K: But I thought you guys were excited to go. I thought there was going to be pizza.

N: It's fine. We will wear dresses and stay here.

K: OK. We can order pizza I guess.

N: And we can dance.

K: Sure, why not.

N: And do adding subtracting. With big numbers.

K: Wow when you guys party you don't fool around.

N: Will you also do?

K: Adding subtracting? Absolutely not.

N: With big numbers?

K: Definitely not with big numbers.

N: You can watch us then.

K: Sure, that sounds like a lot of fun. You're absolutely sure you don't want to go? We still can if you want.

N: No. We stay here. We can do adding subtracting and dance.

K: Sounds like a good time to me.

N: Ya. It will be.

GOOD
MORNING
Homo
Biscuit
TEN CENTS
A PACKAGE
R U for an X ation 2,
My cous N ?—heart and ☞
He off R's in a ¶
A § 2 of land.

Kuzhali Manickavel was born in Winnipeg, Canada, moved to Chidambaram, Tamil Nadu at the age of 13, and now lives in Bengaluru, Karnataka.

Her short fiction collections *Insects Are Just Like You and Me Except Some of Them Have Wings* and *Things We Found During the Autopsy*, as well as several chapbooks, are available from Blaft Publications. Links to more of her work can be found at **kuzhalimanickavel.com**.